More Than Moccasins

A
Kid's Activity Guide
to Traditional
North American Indian
Life

Laurie Carlson

CHICAGO
REVIEW
PRESS

Library of Congress Cataloging-in-Publication Data
Carlson, Laurie., 1952–
        More than moccasins : a kid's activity guide to traditional
North American Indian life / Laurie Carlson.—1st ed.
        p.   cm.
        ISBN 978-1-55652-213-0
        1. Indians of North America—Study and teaching—Activity
Programs—Juvenile literature. I. Title.
E76.6.C37   1994
973'.0497'007—dc20   93-39922
                                                                             CIP
                                                                             AC

The author and the publisher disclaim all liability incurred in connection with the use of the information contained in this book.

Published by Chicago Review Press, Incorporated
814 North Franklin Street
Chicago, Illinois 60610
ISBN 978-1-55652-213-0
Printed in the United States of America

19 18 17 16 15 14

For my grandmothers, Laura and Doris.
Thank you for all that you taught and showed.

"The kind of trail you make will determine success or failure. It is not what you say that counts the most, but it is what you do."
—Anna M. Shaw, Pima

Contents

INTRODUCTION

For thousands of years, the only people that lived in North America were Native Americans. Scientists think that they first came from Asia to Alaska during the Ice Age. They walked across a land bridge that is now covered by the ocean.

They lived here for thousands of years before Columbus and his Spanish ships arrived. The Spaniards were looking for India, so they called the people they met "Indians." The name stuck. It was easier than learning the names of all the Native American groups; there were hundreds of different nations!

The Native Americans lived everywhere: in deserts, on mountains, in valleys, in woodlands, and in swamps. Some farmed, some hunted, some fished, and some were traders.

Early Native Americans lived in small family groups, or tribes, all over North America. Most tribes spoke their own language, had their own customs, and formed many nations across the land.

Years ago, people had to make everything they needed. There were no stores. If they couldn't find what they wanted, they traded for it or found something else to use. The materials they used had to be gathered near their homes because they had to walk everywhere they went.

The kinds of things each tribe used to make tools, clothing, toys, shelter, and food depended upon what they found around them or what they could trade. They didn't try to live in a way that didn't make sense. The people of the Plains, who traveled a lot, didn't make clay pots. Pots were too heavy and broke too easily when they were moved, so they made storage containers and even houses from animal hides.

People who lived in the dry desert Southwest didn't make houses from logs because there weren't many trees. Instead, they created houses from rocks and mud called "pueblos."

In sunny California, the grass grew tall and lush. People there used the grass to weave mats for their houses, clothing to wear, and even watertight baskets to cook in. (They cooked by dropping hot rocks into the basket of stew.)

The Native Americans were resourceful about finding materials to use, and they always tried new ideas and ways to use them. The projects are designed so that you can do that, too. While the real item might have been made from hide, bone, and feathers, those things aren't easy for all of us to find and collect.

So, do as they did! Look around you for other materials to substitute. While you hunt and gather, you'll probably find an endless supply of bathroom tissue tubes, brown paper bags, plastic milk jugs, newspapers, and empty cans. Let your materials speak to you, as early artists did, and feel free to change each project to use what you have on hand.

This book is filled with ideas for fun and interesting things to make that will help you learn about what life was like for Indian children long ago. It will give you a chance to live with history, enjoying it while you create. The projects are designed to make history exciting to explore, using everyday things you find around your home.

Store your supplies in a large box, and add to it whenever you find something with possibilities.

Some items to collect:

Beaded jewelry

Old wigs and hairpieces (Swish in warm water and dish soap, dry on a bath towel, and comb gently.)

Leather clothing

Old fur collars, cuffs, and hats

Leather bootlaces

Sticks (Gather or save popsicle sticks.)

Dowels

Paint and coffee stirrers

Feathers (Feather dusters are a source, or you can gather them in your yard, wash in warm water, shape them, and dry.)

Aluminum pie pans (Recycle them when you are finished.)

Round pizza cardboards

Small stones

Shells

Chamois (Try an auto supply store.)

Vinyl pieces

Yarn scraps

Buttons

Bells

Colored felt

Ribbons and sewing trims

Brown paper bags

Paper towel and bathroom tissue tubes

Thread spools

Small pieces of bone (Save from dinner, soak in vinegar, and scrub with a toothbrush.)

The projects in this book will help you understand the people who made the items and how they lived. Some items can be found in museums, and some are still being made by Native Americans today.

Feel free to do as the Indian artist did—add or change the designs to better use the materials you have, or to show your own creativity.

Indians were always eager to find new materials and ideas, choosing and using what they felt to be more elegant, unique or useful. Let your own projects reflect that same spirit!

There are about 500 tribes in North America today. A tribe is a group of relatives who speak the same language and have the same leader, or chief. A chief can be a man or woman.

There are about 2 million American Indians, Eskimos, and Aleuts in the United States.
Today, 800,000 Indians live on or near reservations; 1,200,000 live in cities and suburbs.

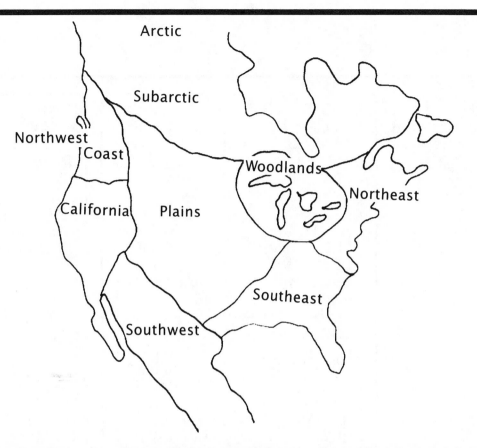

NORTH AMERICAN INDIAN CULTURE MAP

This map shows where the people had similar lifestyles. The people that lived in each area had food, clothes, art, and languages similar to their neighbors.

HOW TO SAY IT!
The names of many tribes are hard to pronounce. This may help you with the unusual ones.

ALEUTS	Al-ee-oots
ALGONQUIAN	Algone-key-un
ANASAZI	Ann-uh-saw-zee
APACHE	Uh-patch-ee
ARAPAHO	Uh-rap-uh-hoe
ARIKARA	Uh-ree-kuh-ruh
BANNOCK	Ban-ek
BELLA COOLA	Bella Cool-uh
CHEROKEE	Chair-oh-kee
CHEYENNE	Shy-ann
CHIPPEWA	Chip-uh-wah
CHIRICAHUA APACHE	
Cheer-uh-caw-wah Uh-patch-ee	
CHOCTAW	Chock-taw
COCOPAS	Ko-ko-paw
COEUR D'ALENE	Core-duh-lane
DAKOTA	Duh-koh-tah
HAIDA	Hi-duh
HAVASUPAI	Have-uh-soup-eye
HIDATSA	Hi-dot-suh
HOHOKAM	Ho-ho-kahm
HOPI	Hope-ee
HUPA	Hoo-paw
HURON	Hyou-ron
IROQUOIS	Ear-oh-kwoy
KIOWA	Ki-oh-wah
KUTENAI	Koo-ten-ay

MIWOK	Mee-wuk
MOHAVE	Mo-hah-vee
MOHEGAN	Mo-hee-gun
NAVAJO	Na-va-hoe
NEZ PERCE	Nezz Purse
OJIBWA	Oh-jib-wah
OMAHA	Oh-muh-hah
ONEIDA	On-ni-dah
ONONDAGA	Oh-nen-dog-uh
PAIUTE	Pie-yute
PAPAGO	Paw-paw-go
PAWNEE	Paw-nee
PIEGAN	Pie-ee-gun
PIMA	Pee-mah
POMO	Poh-moh
SHOSHONE	Show-show-nee
SIOUX	Sue or Soo
TETON	Tee-tawn
TLINGET	Tling-get
TSIMSYAN	Sim-shin
UMATILLA	You-mah-tilla
UTE	Yoot
YAKIMA	Yack-uh-maw
YOKUT	Yo-cut
YUMA	You-mah
YUROK	Your-rock
ZUNI	Zoo-nee

NOTE TO GROWN-UPS

We realize the importance of recognizing and learning about the many different people that make up our world. As parents and teachers, we can open a child's eyes to history and cultures—their own and those of others. We can create knowledge and interest in the variety of customs and heritages each of us have. The people who first settled the continent have left us many legacies. The ideas and traditions of the Native American people can enrich and excite children, teaching them about the many different people and beliefs that are part of our nation.

The purpose of this book is not to "become an Indian," but to discover, learn, and enjoy activities that are a large part of our country's heritage. The ideas here will give children a fun, hands-on historical and cultural experience.

Indian arts and crafts are our only truly native culture. Using bone, grass, shell, antlers, and other simple materials, Native Americans created artistic expression unequaled anywhere in the world. Their creations were as fine and elegant as any ever made.

They were successful because they were so finely tuned to the natural environment. They respected the natural sources of their materials. They didn't overuse or abuse the natural world around them because they depended upon it for survival.

The things a culture makes tell much about its people. Things made by Native American individuals followed the general style of the tribe, but showed individuality as well. They followed tradition, but were experimenting all the time, too.

They were very social and eagerly exchanged ideas and goods with other groups. If they liked a new technique, they refined it to fit their own traditions and adopted it.

The materials that were available dictated what could be made, but human creativity did the rest.

EVERYDAY LIFE

Long ago, Indian families had everyday lives much like we do today. Homes had to be built and kept tidy. Treasures and tools had to be stored away carefully. Food had to be cooked, and clothing wore out and had to be replaced. People found different ways to do these things, depending upon what the weather and land was like where they lived.

Whether they lived in traveling camps or large villages, aunts, uncles, cousins, and grandparents all lived nearby; an Indian child was never lonely.

> **Fast Fact** A good hunter could get 10 arrows in the air before one had fallen to the ground.

Tepee

The Indians on the Plains hunted the huge herds of buffalo that roamed the grasslands. They used the meat, hides, and bones to make almost everything they needed. The buffalo didn't stay in one place but roamed around looking for grass to eat. The people had to follow them, so the Indians built portable houses that could be moved quickly and easily.

The Dakota people called their beautiful portable homes tepees. They made them from buffalo skins held up by poles. It took between 10 and 40 hides for one tepee, depending upon how wealthy the family was. New tepees were made in the spring to replace old ones that had worn out.

The outside of a tepee was decorated with paint. The top could be held open with poles to let smoke from the fire escape or it could be closed to keep out the rain. In the summer, the bottom could be rolled up to let a cool breeze pass through.

Each spring, all the members of a tribe gathered at one great camp. A council tepee was built in the center and the different bands or family groups put their tepees in a circle around it. Each band had a certain section of the circle so that people could find each other easily. A person would always know where to find an old friend because his or her tepee would be in the same place each spring. After all, they didn't have street signs or house numbers, and these great camps had hundreds of tepees and thousands of people!

When women gathered together to work on a new tepee, they enjoyed a special feast. It took about a day for them to make a new one. When it was time to move the tepees, the women did the work, too. In contests, two Indian women could put up a tepee in less than three minutes! When it was time to move, the tepee was rolled up and tied to a "travois," along with the other things to be moved. The travois was made out of two poles that were fastened to the sides of a horse, a person, or a dog and pulled along the ground.

> **Fast Fact** The Crow tribe had some tepee lodges so large that 40 men could dine together in one.

> **Good Idea** Some families made small "dog house" tepees for their pet dog. When it was time to move on, the dog's tepee was taken down and tied onto a travois that the dog pulled to the next camp.
>
> **Kids' Stuff** Mothers made toy tepees for their daughters to play with. That's how a girl learned to take down and set up her family's home.

You can make a toy tepee, or an entire encampment!

MATERIALS

Bowl or plate
Construction paper
Markers, crayons, or paint
Scissors
Tape

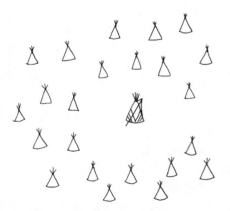

The camp was set up around the council tepee.

 Draw a large circle of paper by tracing around the rim of a bowl or plate. Cut the circle out and then cut it in half.

Decorate half the circle with interesting, pretty designs. Roll it into a cone shape and tape or glue the ends together. Cut a slit and fold back the door flaps. Make some clay people to live inside. (Use Play Clay, page 69.)

New tepees were white, but darkened gradually at the top from smoke. Use brown crayon to darken the top part.

Make several to create a whole spring camp!

What kind of furniture was inside a tepee? Only simple, lightweight things that could be carried from camp to camp. Tree boughs were piled and covered with hides for beds.

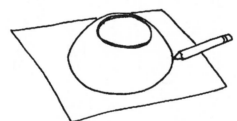

Use a bowl to trace a large circle.

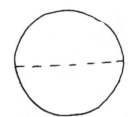

Cut the circle in half.

Roll into a cone and tape. Fold back the door flaps.

Decorate and build an entire village.

Backrest

Backrests were made by weaving willow branches together. Furs were piled on top so that they were comfortable for people relaxing in their special places in the rear of the tepee and behind the fire.

MATERIALS

Construction paper
3 toothpicks
Scissors
Markers
Glue

You can make a tiny backrest for your tepee by cutting paper in the shape shown. Decorate it with markers and fold it. Use the toothpicks for the supports. Poke the narrow ends of the toothpicks into the top of the backrest. Glue 2 of the toothpicks securely to the back of the backrest. Spread the third toothpick back for support, like a tripod.

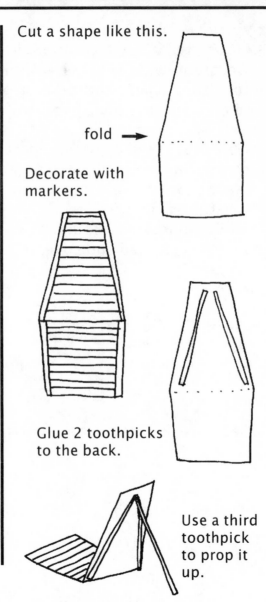

Cut a shape like this.

fold →

Decorate with markers.

Glue 2 toothpicks to the back.

Use a third toothpick to prop it up.

Good Manners People were careful to never walk in front of someone sitting in the tepee. It was a very rude thing to do. Instead, the people who were seated leaned forward so that others could pass behind them.

Good Manners The Sioux people signaled when visitors were welcome. If a neighbor's tepee flap was open, a visitor was welcome. If the flap was down, a visitor had to rattle it a bit and wait to be invited in. If the flap was closed and 2 sticks were crossed over the door, no visitors were welcome.

Fast Fact All chiefs had runners or criers who ran through the camp announcing the chief's decision to move camp. When the chief's tepee started to be taken down, it signaled everyone to begin. A visitor to an early Sioux camp saw some 600 tepees taken down in only a few minutes.

Wigwam

Many tribes lived in villages that stayed in one place. They didn't travel as much as the Plains tribes. People in the Great Lakes area, the East, and California built houses and lived near lakes or rivers. Many of them planted gardens and sold the vegetables to explorers and fur traders. Wigwam-type houses were built by Indians in many areas across the country. They used young trees that could be cut to make poles that bent easily into the framework. The poles were covered with whatever was available—peeled bark, woven grass mats, mud, twigs, and branches.

Indians built the frame of the wigwam by burying the ends of the saplings in the ground, bending them, and then lashing them together with strips of bark or hide. The covering was tied on in bundles. A hole was left in the roof near the center so that smoke from the fire in the center pit could escape.

MATERIALS

Sheet of paper, 8½ by 11 inches
Coffee filter
Brown paper bag
Scissors
Glue
Tape
Watercolor paints or crayons

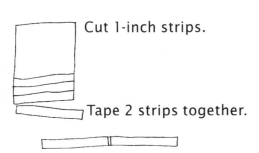
Cut 1-inch strips.

Tape 2 strips together.

Tape it into a loop.

Tape 3 strips to the loop to make a frame.

Cover with a coffee filter.

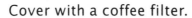

Cut the paper into 1-inch strips. Tape 2 of the strips together to make a long piece. Tape it into a loop to use as the base. Tape 3 strips to make a frame. Use paint or crayons to make the coffee filter brown, green, or tan to match whatever you want to cover it with. Glue it over the framework. Cut a door opening, and fold it back. Glue on leaves, grass clippings, or cut paper strips to cover the coffee filter with a natural-looking roof.

You can also cover your wigwam with torn strips of brown paper bag, dipped in glue. Let it dry hard.

13

Glue grass or straw to the coffee filter.

Good Manners *In tepees and wigwams, every family member had a special place to sit or sleep. Usually the father or the eldest adults sat in the honored place in the rear, behind the fire. This was a nice spot because no draft blew from the door and it was the least smoky place to sit.*

You can also dip torn strips of paper in paste and layer them.

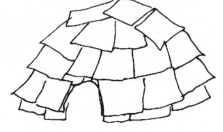

paste

Pueblo Village

The desert dwellers in the Southwest created beautiful and practical homes from mud. They formed walls out of building blocks made from a mixture of clay, water, and straw and covered with smooth layers of mud. This kind of house was perfect for the hot, dry climate in the Southwest.

Early explorers called the mud bricks "adobe" (uh-dough-bee), a Spanish word. These adobe buildings were sometimes like big apartment buildings. The Indians built them on top of a flat hill so that they could watch for enemies. When they built the first level, they used logs as beams for the ceiling. They covered the logs with layers of grass and twigs and a thick layer of adobe mud. When it was dry, the next level was built right on top of the first. Each level had several rooms. A large family would live on one level, with grandparents, aunts, uncles, and cousins living in the many rooms. A different family lived on the level above or below. There was a platform around each level—a deck—where ladders were set.

To keep enemies from getting in, the first-floor rooms had no doors. Those who lived there climbed ladders and went inside through a hole in the roof. When enemies were coming, the people pulled all the ladders inside.

You can make a single pueblo house from a shoe box or join someone else to make a large village from many boxes.

MATERIALS

Cardboard boxes in
various sizes
Moss or green sponges
Cornmeal, salt, or sand
Black construction paper
Twigs or popsicle sticks
Tan tempera or
latex house paint
Craft glue (or a hot glue gun,
for grown-up use)
Scissors

Arrange the boxes with the larger ones on the bottom. Glue them together in position. It is easier if you have a large, flat cardboard base to attach them to so that you can pick up and move the village easily. You can add desert plants by gluing pieces of moss or green sponges to the base.

Use pointed scissors to cut roof openings here and there. Since, the pueblo people built the first story without doorways, they had to climb ladders and go inside through door-

15

ways in the roof. When an enemy approached, they could pull up the ladders to keep the enemy from getting inside.

Paint all the boxes the same shade of light tan. Before the paint dries, sprinkle cornmeal, salt, or fine sand on it for an adobe effect.

Cut rectangles from black paper and glue on for windows and doors.

Make ladders from twigs or popsicle sticks.

Use "Play Clay" (see page 69) to make the outdoor cooking ovens called "hornos." They were shaped like beehives and made from clay and mud. Women baked bread in these every day. Make a few small cooking and water pots, too.

Glue sticks together to make ladders.

Make ovens from clay.

Weaving

People have been weaving baskets in North America for more than 8,000 years. Most Indian tribes made some kind of basket.

Basket making was always done by women. They made sure to gather the finest supplies and prepare them carefully before starting a basket. They used whatever plants they could gather— roots, grass, cedar or oak splints, corn husks, bark strips, fern stems, cattail stems, and horsehair.

They made baskets to carry and store food in. Some baskets were woven so tightly that they could hold water! Baskets were used to cook food in, too. A rock was heated in the fire, lifted with sticks, and then dropped into a basket of soup or mush to cook it. Baskets were also used as baby cradles, hats, and traps for fish or birds.

Papago women in the Southwest made baskets with black lines striped around them. They often borrowed food from each other for their family's meal. They could refill a basket to the same black line when returning it. The women were very generous with each other, but food was hard to get in the harsh desert.

MATERIALS

Newspaper
Potato
Scissors
Stapler
Glue
Knife and spoon
Tempera paint

❀ Cut a large double sheet of newspaper down the middle fold, and then cut it in half crosswise. Fold the sheet lengthwise 3 times. Staple once in the center to hold its shape, or use a bit of glue to keep it from unfolding.

Make 16 folded strips, each about 1½ by 12 inches. Staple 9 strips next to each other along 1 strip. Weave other strips over and under these, stapling around the outer edges. Trim the ends with the scissors so that they are even.

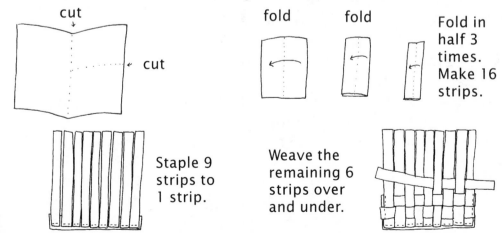

cut

cut

fold   fold   Fold in half 3 times. Make 16 strips.

Staple 9 strips to 1 strip.

Weave the remaining 6 strips over and under.

The Indians in the New England area, like the Mohegans, used long flat pieces split from hardwood tree logs. They used potatoes and paint to stamp designs on their finished baskets. You can decorate your woven mat the same way. Cut a raw potato in half. Use a spoon or knife to carve out a design, then press the potato into bright tempera paint and stamp your design all over the woven mat. The Indians would have used berry paints for theirs.

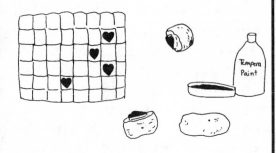

Print designs with potato shapes and paint.

Basket

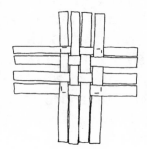 Instead of tagboard, you can use newspaper. Cut full sheets of newspaper apart at the center fold. Fold each piece lengthwise 3 times and put a bit of glue along the crease to hold its shape. Lay down 4 strips, all in the same direction. Weave 4 more strips over and under them, pushing all the strips close together in the center. Staple them together at the corners. Fold and crease all the strips to turn upwards. This will give the basket its shape. When you get to the end of a strip, staple another one over it. For the last row at the top, bend and staple strips along the edge.

Interesting effects can be created using 2 colors of tagboard or using the colored comics sections from the newspaper.

Lay 4 strips side by side.

MATERIALS

14 strips of tagboard,
20 by 1 inches
Stapler
Scissors

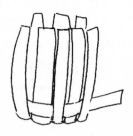

Weave 4 more strips over and under. Staple the corners.

Fold the strips up. Weave the rest of the strips over and under.

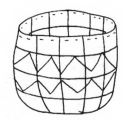

Fold and staple the ends when finished. Paint it.

18

Burden Basket

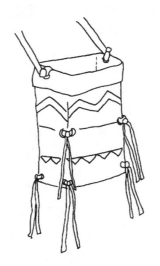

Women in the Southwest and California tribes wove large, cone-shaped baskets that they used to carry firewood and wild foods. The baskets hung on their back from a band that went around their forehead or over their shoulders called a "tumpline." They wove their burden baskets with care and decorated them with deerskin fringes, shells, and beads. They prized their baskets because they were not only beautiful but they made their hard work easier.

Fast Fact *Tumplines made it possible for a girl to carry very heavy loads because she used the strong muscles of her neck and balanced the load evenly against her back.*

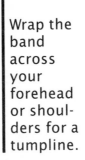

Wrap the band across your forehead or shoulders for a tumpline.

MATERIALS

Brown paper bag, lunch- to medium-sized
Yarn
Beads, uncooked macaroni, or cutout paper shells
Hole punch
Scissors
Markers or crayons

Fold the top of the bag down about 1 or 2 inches. Punch a hole in each side. Tie on a length of yarn that can ride easily across your forehead or shoulders. You can try it against your forehead, but it might be easier for you across your shoulders. Decorate it with markers or crayons. Punch holes along the sides and bottom of the bag, punching along the creases to make 2 holes at a time. Thread lengths of yarn through the holes. Tie on beads, macaroni, or cutout paper shells. Wear the basket on your back with the tumpline across your shoulders or forehead.

Pottery

lmost every Indian tribe made pottery. Pots were made from clay that was shaped by hand and hardened by baking in a fire. Each Indian group made a different type of pot. Pots break easily, but the pieces, called "potsherds," can last a long time. Archeologists have dated the oldest pots in North America at almost 4,000 years old.

Women usually were the pot makers. They would dig clay from the same place each year. The clay was dried and crushed into very small pieces. Pebbles and twigs were picked out. The clay was as smooth as flour. When she was ready to make pots, the potter added water to the clay dust until it was like dough. Small amounts of limestone, ground shells, sand, or plant fibers were kneaded into the soft clay. This kept the clay from cracking as the pot was dried and baked in a fire.

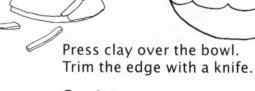

Cover a bowl with aluminum foil.

Press clay over the bowl. Trim the edge with a knife.

Roll a clay rope.

Continue coiling to make a pot.

Wrap it in a coil.

Smooth with finger-tips and a bit of water.

MATERIALS

Clay
(Go to an art or ceramic supply store, or dig some of your own!)
Aluminum foil
Cereal bowl or a clean margarine tub
Small bowl of water
Table knife
Newspaper

You'll need access to a kiln if you want to fire the pot. Ceramics shops will do the firing for you very inexpensively.

Cherokee, Papago, Yuma, Mandan, and Anasazi potters used baskets or old pots to shape the wet clay to create new pots. Use a cereal bowl or margarine tub to form your pot.

Turn the bowl upside down and cover it with aluminum foil pressed tightly in place.

Press the clay flat to make a large pancake. Lay it over the outside of the bowl. Press the clay against the bowl, forming it into the shape of the bowl. Use a knife to trim the edge evenly. Let the clay dry on the bowl until it is firm. Gently remove it from the bowl and foil and set it to dry on newspaper. Set it on its base so that air circulates inside the pot.

Some Indian potters made their pots by rolling clay into long coils. Roll a lump of clay between your palms to make a "rope" as thick as your finger. Wrap the clay rope around and around to make a bowl shape. Keep rolling new pieces of rope as you need it. Use your fingers to press the coils smooth. Wet your fingertips with a bit of water to smooth the clay if it begins to dry.

Let the pot dry completely, and then fire it in a kiln. A ceramics shop can do this for you. Indian potters didn't always fire their pots, but if they weren't fired they broke easily and wouldn't hold water without leaking. To fire pots, they dug a pit in the ground, piled the pots in it, and covered it with earth. A fire was built over it. Pots weren't removed until the fire burned out and everything cooled.

Indians decorated their pots in many different ways. The potters of each tribe used the same kind of designs and paints, but each person tried to make hers a bit different.

Indians gathered plants and cooked them to make paints. They also dug colored clays and mixed them with water.

The paint was put on the pot with sticks, tufts of fur, feathers, or yucca stem brushes. To make a brush from a yucca stem, the potter would gently chew on one end until it was soft and feathery.

Pots could also be decorated while the clay was still soft. Potters in the Eastern and ancient Southwest tribes pressed or poked designs on the pot before the clay dried. They used shells, sticks, or fingernails on the soft clay.

You can use toothpicks, hair pins, screws, bolts, buttons, or whatever else is handy, to press interesting designs on your pot before it dries hard.

Native Wisdom *Zuni potters put a tiny bit of corn bread in each pot before firing it. They thought the pot's spirit would be able to feast on the bread. This was thought to give life and health to any food later put into the pot.*

Ancient Ancestors *The Mimbres people of the prehistoric Southwest buried bowls with the dead owners. The bowl was "killed" by poking a hole through the bottom—perhaps this released the spirit from the bowl or kept anyone else from using the special bowl.*

If you don't have clay to make pots you can shape them from homemade salt dough and let them air dry. Paint them with tempera or watercolors. Here's a simple recipe for salt dough:

4 cups flour
1½ cups water
1 cup salt
Food coloring (optional)

Mix all the ingredients together in a bowl. Add more water or flour to make a dough that holds its shape but doesn't stick to your hands. Mold it into small pots. Let it dry a few days, and then paint as you like. You can use food coloring to tint the water before you make the dough to give your pots some color.

You can also make papier-mâché bowls by dipping torn strips of newspaper in a flour-and-water paste. Layer the wet strips over a plastic bowl or margarine tub that has

been coated with a petroleum jelly (like Vaseline). When dry, pop it off the plastic bowl. Trim the rim evenly with scissors. Paint with tempera paints.

Scratch designs in the soft clay.

Sample designs to paint.

Another way you can enjoy creating pottery designs without clay, is by using disposable paper bowls. Buy them in the picnic section of the grocery store. Draw designs on them with colorful markers. Don't color inside the bowls if you plan to eat from them.

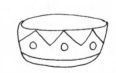

Cover a bowl with petroleum jelly. Layer it with torn paper strips dipped in paste.

Dry, trim edges, and paint.

Boxes

Just as we do now, Indians of the past needed somewhere to store their food, tools, fancy clothes, and special treasures.

Woodland people used tree bark to make boxes. Plains people used hides. They were stiff, sturdy, and not as heavy as pottery, and they wouldn't break during the frequent moves tepee dwellers had to make.

The boxes were cut from bark or heavy rawhide, folded into shape, and stitched or tied together with strips of hide or sinew. The outsides were painted with bright, colorful designs.

You can make a simple box just like they did, using heavy paper instead of bark or hide.

MATERIALS

Posterboard, construction paper, or brown paper bag
Yarn
Scissors
Hole punch
Markers or paint

Photocopy the pattern. Use it the same size or enlarge it to the size you want. Cut along the solid lines. Fold along the broken lines. Punch holes for the yarn ties.

Fold in the sides first, and then thread a yarn piece through both sets of holes and tie.

Fold one end over first, and then the other. Thread yarn pieces through each matching set of holes. Tie.

Decorate with geometric designs in bright colors.

Cut out the pattern and draw lines to make it look like bark.

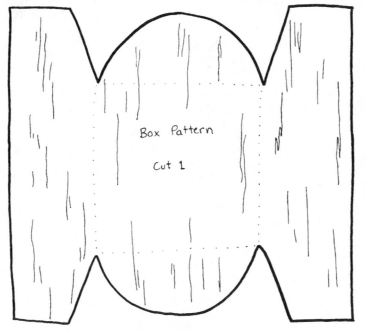

Box Pattern

Cut 1

Cut on solid lines. Fold on dotted lines. Glue ends together.

Parfleche

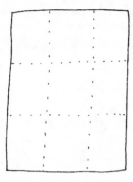

Fold a rectangle in thirds lengthwise and crosswise. Open.

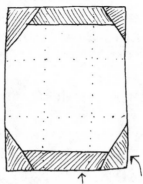

Trim the corners and ends on the solid lines.

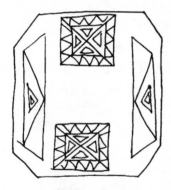

Decorate.

Fold up. Punch 2 holes at each end, thread yarn through, and tie closed.

MATERIALS

Construction paper, tagboard, or brown paper bag
4 pieces of yarn, 6 inches long
Scissors
Crayons or markers
Hole punch
Markers or crayons, or fabric paints for cloth

Cut the paper into a rectangle. You can make it any size you like. Fold it in thirds lengthwise and crosswise, and then open it up.

Trim off the corners and ends. Decorate with crayons or markers. The Plains people used geometric shapes, such as triangles, diamonds, and lines.

Fold it along the creases. Punch 2 holes on each end, thread yarn through the holes, and tie it closed.

Say it: "parflesh." Plains Indians made large hide envelopes to store food and clothing. They were easy to store inside the tepee and could be hung from the tepee poles. They could be stacked on a travois for moving.

24

Bark Containers

Indians that lived around the Great Lakes area, such as the Chippewa and Cree, used the bark from birch trees to make many things. They used birch bark to cover their wigwams, make canoes, and create basket-like pails. Birch bark is almost waterproof and pots made from bark could be used for cooking. Hot stones were dropped into the stew or the bark pot could be hung over a fire as long as there was liquid in it.

Bark was used to make buckets, boxes, trays, bowls, and cups.

Make a simple folded pan, like those used by Chippewa children to catch maple syrup or gather wild rice. Theirs were made from birch bark.

Depending on Plants *Birch bark was very valuable to people living in the Great Lakes area. The Chippewa people could split the bark of large trees into six to nine layers. They used thick bark to make strong canoes that could carry several people. Thin bark was used to wrap foods. Whatever is stored in birch bark will not decay. Containers for holding food—even maple syrup—were made from bark.*

MATERIALS

Light tan construction paper or tagboard, or brown paper bag
Pencil
Scissors
Glue

 Draw and cut out your tray like the shape shown. It can be any size. Fold the paper on the dotted lines. Unfold and cut away the corners. Glue the corners over each other.

Open and cut away the corners along the creases.

C

Color and draw lines to look like bark.

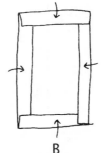 Fold in all sides 2 inches.

A

Fold the sides up and glue the corners over each other.

B

Pouch

Cut out A.
Decorate with flower
designs like Woodland
people did.

Cut out B.

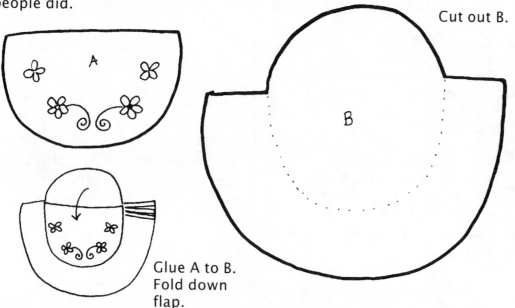

Glue A to B.
Fold down
flap.

People of every tribe used small bags or pouches to carry things in. They had pouches to hold everyday things like sewing tools and special ones to carry pipes or body paints used in ceremonies. "Strike-a-light" pouches were used to carry flint for making fire—something every home needed. Pouches were made from the soft skin of an animal. Plains people decorated their pouches with geometric designs. Woodland people made flower designs.

Make a small pouch to hold something special for yourself.

MATERIALS

Chamois, felt, leatherlike material, or construction paper
Beads, felt scraps, braid trim, or the decoration of your choice
Scissors
Glue, or a needle and thread
Acrylic paints, markers, or crayons

Use the pattern shown to make a pouch. Cut out the 2 pieces and glue or sew A to B as shown. Cut a fringe with scissors. Decorate with acrylic paints, markers, or crayons. Sew or glue on old buttons or beads.

If you want to wear your pouch on a belt, cut 2 slits in the back of the pouch to thread the belt through.

Cut fringe.

26

Canoe

People living near rivers or lakes built small boats from what-ever was available. They used reeds, sewn skins, hollowed-out tree trunks, or tree bark. The Iroquois made canoes from elm or spruce bark fastened to a wooden frame. Canoes were very lightweight and easy to carry.

The canoe was controlled with wooden paddles. When travel became difficult, the canoe was light enough to be carried on land—or "portaged."

The canoe made travel easier and was used for fishing and hunting.

When not being used, an upside-down canoe could be used to cover the smoke hole of a wigwam. It could also be used as a lad-der or as a shield when fighting an enemy.

MATERIALS

2 thin Styrofoam trays
(from meat or bakery prod-ucts) or thin cardboard
Yarn, 2 feet long
Pencil
Scissors
Hole punch or large nail

❁ Use the pattern to draw 2 canoe shapes on the clean foam trays. Cut them out. Punch holes around the side and bot-tom edges of both pieces.

Wrap a piece of tape around an end of the yarn so that it won't unravel while you push it through the holes.

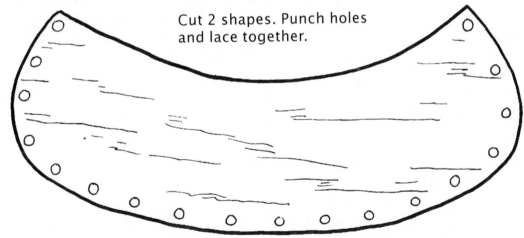

Cut 2 shapes. Punch holes and lace together.

Wrap tape on end of yarn for reinforcement; this will make it easier to lace through the holes.

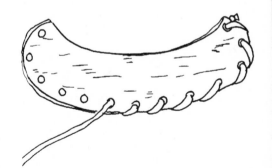

Fishing Lure

Fish were an important food for Indian families. They were caught in many different ways. Some people made hand-knotted nets or traps made from sticks. Some built dams with rocks, dirt, and fallen trees and scooped fish from the water with baskets.

Some tribes in the Southwest used special plants to catch fish. They ground up buckeye nuts, pokeweed, or walnut bark and tossed the powder into the water of a small pool or pond. The poison stunned the fish so that they floated to the top of the water and the people could pick them up easily.

Feather Lure

Shell Spinner

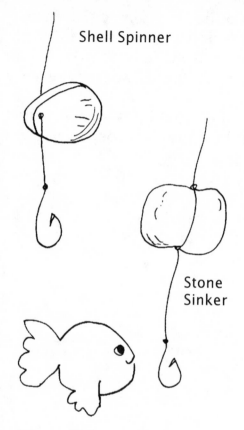

Stone Sinker

Some fishermen tied a lure made of feathers to a line and dangled it in the water. When a fish came up to it, the fish was speared.

Indians made fishhooks from bones, antlers, shells, wood, and even cactus spines.

To make a simple lure, tie some small feathers together and attach them to the fishing line an inch above your fishhook.

If you have a small flat shell, ask an adult to drill a hole in it at one end. Thread your fishing line through the hole and it will act like a spinner.

A stone can be tied onto your line for a sinker.

Do like the Iroquois: cut a 1-to-2-inch section from a corncob. Poke a hole through the center with a nail, then thread it onto the fishing line to use as a float.

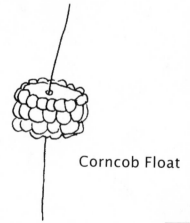

Corncob Float

Duck Decoy

Indian men made hunting decoys for two reasons: to lure ducks closer while hunting and to use when teaching young boys hunting skills.

You can make simple duck decoys that will float jauntily on a pond or lake, or in a bathtub.

MATERIALS

Cattail leaves
String
Scissors

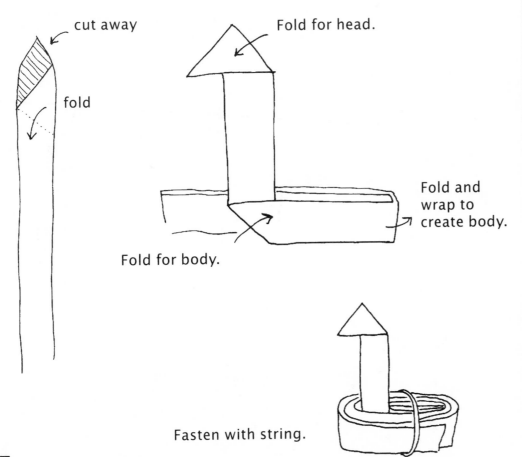

cut away

fold

Fold for head.

Fold and wrap to create body.

Fold for body.

Fasten with string.

✿ Use a long, straight cattail leaf. If you can't find one, cut a long strip of heavy paper (a brown paper bag) that is 2 inches wide and fold it in half to make a strong 1-inch strip.

To make the duck's head, cut 1 corner of the leaf away. Fold the leaf diagonally as shown. Fold again, about 2 inches below the first fold. Then begin folding and wrapping the leaf to make the duck's body. If you need to add another cattail leaf, slip it under the first leaf and continue. When you have it as thick as you want (or at least 2 inches wide), tie the folds together tightly with string.

Try floating your duck on a pond. If you wait quietly behind some rushes, perhaps a wild duck will swim up to yours!

Good Idea *Indians living in the Nevada area made duck decoys hundreds of years ago. They stuffed the feathered skins of birds or carved them from wood. They also made them from rushes, feathers, and paint. They used the fake floating ducks to lure ducks to a pond, where they waited quietly to hunt them.*

Native Wisdom *Some hunters were good at catching ducks and geese by swimming beneath them in the water using a hollow reed for breathing like a snorkel. Some could float among the swimming ducks with a gourd over their heads and get close enough to catch the ducks.*

Special Shield

A warrior made and used a shield for protection. It could be held during battle to deflect arrows (and even some bullets) from attackers. It was also thought to give spiritual protection to its owner.

A man made his shield carefully and usually decorated it with designs he had dreamed about. Special feathers and small bags of precious stones or amulets were tied onto the shield for good luck.

The shield was displayed in a special place in the home and was usually buried with the man when he died.

Make your own special shield to hang on the wall of your room.

thunderbird

buffalo

turtle

MATERIALS

2 paper plates
Colorful crepe-paper streamers
Colored paper scraps
for feathers
Scissors
Markers, crayons, or paints
Stapler

Cut out a strip 2 inches wide from 1 plate for the handle. Decorate the other with bright colors in a design that means something special to you. Decorate the base of the plate, as it will be the front of the shield. Staple the handle to the back of the decorated plate, at the sides.

Staple on a few paper streamers and feathers cut from colored paper.

Decorate one plate.
Cut the other plate for a 2-inch strip.

Staple it to the back of the shield.

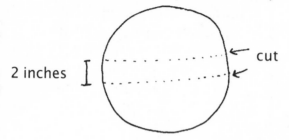

2 inches

← cut
←

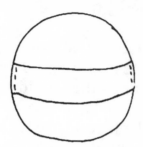

Staple on paper feathers and streamers.

Fast Fact *Plains warriors carried shields to give them additional powers in battle. The drawings on the shields were chosen to provide special powers: Bears meant strength, tortoises were long life, and birds represented swiftness.*

Ancient Ancestors *We don't know who first used the bow and arrow in North America. For 30,000 years, people used the spear, and then in about the year 500 A.D., hunters began making and using bows and arrows. Hunters in Asia and Europe had already been using bows and arrows for over 5,000 years.*

Fast Fact *Warriors tried to capture shields in battle. This meant that a man who carried one was more likely to be attacked.*

Coup Stick

MATERIALS

Stick, about 1 inch thick and
any length you choose
Fake fur, felt, or
red cloth scraps
Feathers
Yarn
Glue
Paint

Create your own style and type of coup stick to hang on your wall. Cut strips from the red cloth and wrap and glue them around the stick, or paint stripes around the stick. Wrap and glue strips of fake fur or colorful felt. Use pieces of yarn to tie on feathers here and there.

Wrap tape in
a spiral.

> **Native Wisdom** In many tribes, the highest honor that could be won was that given for touching a live enemy with the bare hand or a coup stick. Killing or scalping an enemy won less honors. It required more courage to touch an enemy and leave him unhurt than to attack him.

Plains warriors like the Dakota, Crow, Pawnee, Cheyenne, Arapaho, and Kiowa took coup sticks with them into battle. "Coup" is French for "a hit" and rhymes with blue. We often use the word to mean a sudden, successful move.

The warriors used the coup stick to touch live enemies—not to kill them. A warrior who got close enough to an enemy to touch him with a coup stick was considered far braver than one who killed him with a bow and arrow from a distance. An eagle feather could be earned for each coup in battle.

Some daring warriors went into battle armed with only their coup stick!

There were war societies in the Plains called Kit Foxes and Crazy Dogs. They were clubs that met and decided how points could be earned by members counting coup. They were like today's sports teams.

Coup sticks were about the same height as the man. They were decorated with feathers, fur, and beads.

Wampum

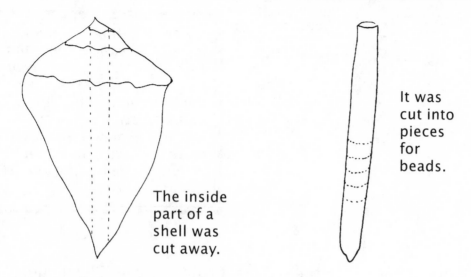

The inside part of a shell was cut away.

It was cut into pieces for beads.

MATERIALS

Uncooked macaroni
Blue and red food coloring
Rubbing alcohol (or water)
Yarn or string, about
18 inches long
Small bowl
Spoon
Newspaper

Pour about 1 cup of alcohol (or water) into the bowl. Add blue and red food coloring a few drops at a time until it becomes a nice bluish purple. Soak half of the macaroni until it is tinted the color you want. If you are using water, don't let the macaroni soak too long; they will get gummy and stick together. Leave it in the tinted water only long enough to color it. Spoon the macaroni out and let it dry on newspaper. Leave the other half of the macaroni untinted.

Indian tribes used shell beads the same way we use money today. The small beads they used were carved from the inner purple and white parts of clam shells. They were tiny and difficult to cut with stone tools. Fewer purple beads could be cut from a shell than white ones, so purple ones were worth twice as much. The beads were strung together and used in trading and making treaties.

The Algonquian and Iroquois introduced wampum as a form of money when trading with settlers. The first settlers didn't have much money to use, so they used strings of purple or white Indian wampum for money. Dutch settlers even began to make wampum in small factories.

Indians often used the beads as jewelry or decoration to show off their wealth. They also wore their beads because they didn't have safes or bank vaults to store them in.

Make your own strings of wampum.

Now you can string your "money" onto the yarn or string. Tie the ends together and wear it as a necklace, like the Indians did.

Tribes on the West Coast used small white dentalium shells for money, instead. They traded the shells with other tribes, who used them for jewelry and clothing decoration.

Knot the string around the first bead to keep the others from sliding off as you work.

Holes were made with a hand tool for drilling.

A pointed stone was tied to the end.

Peace Pipe

Indians were the first to use tobacco. Early explorers were surprised when they first saw Indian people smoking pipes.

The Indians smoked pipes and tobacco as a sacred way to bring good and to stop evil. Pipes were smoked to prevent storms or to bring good luck in a hunt. They were smoked to bring peace and friendship.

The Woodland tribes, like the Algonquian, used pipes first, and then others began to use them.

Tribes made pipes from whatever was easy to find. Some carved them from soft stone, shaped them from clay, or used an animal's leg bone. Men decorated their pipes with quills and feathers. Each tribe's pipes were made a certain way, and others could recognize them.

A man kept his pipe in a special skin bag decorated with beads and fringe. It hung in a special place in the home.

You can make one to display, too. Of course it won't be for smoking!

MATERIALS

Paper towel tube
Bathroom tissue tube
Feathers (real or
cut from paper)
Yarn
Beads
Scissors
Tape
Glue
Markers or paint

Cut out 2 triangles across from each other at one end of the longer tube. Make each about 1½ inches long. Press the cut edges together and fasten them with tape to make a mouthpiece. Cut the smaller tube as shown to make a bowl for the pipe.

Glue the bowl to the pipe. Decorate with markers or paint. Tie on feathers, yarn tassels, or a few beads.

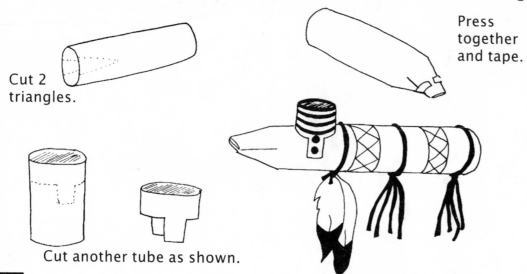

Cut 2 triangles.

Press together and tape.

Cut another tube as shown.

Plant a Garden

Gather your tools.

Plant the seeds in little hills.

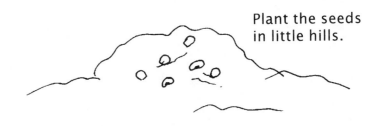

Indian families in the Woodlands, the East, the Southwest, and the northern Plains planted gardens long before settlers came. In fact, they showed the settlers how to plant foods such as corn, beans, and squash that saved many of them from starvation.

You can create a small garden in your backyard. You'll need garden tools like a shovel, rake, and trowel. (Indian farmers used digging sticks.) In the spring, dig and turn the soil until it's loose. Pick out all the weeds, grass, sticks, and stones. Rake it smooth. Use the trowel to create a little hill. Plant a few corn seeds and bean seeds in each hill. The corn will grow tall and the bean plants will "climb" up the corn stalks for support. Plant squash in other little hills. Follow the directions on the seed packets and you'll enjoy a bountiful harvest!

Indians also grew pumpkins, melons, and gourds. Why not try them, too?

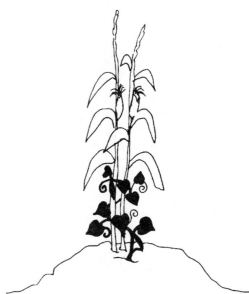

Bean plants will grow up corn stalks.

THINGS TO WEAR

Indian people living in different areas of North America wore different types of clothing and jewelry. What they wore depended upon the weather and what materials they could find. Children living in warm desert areas wore practically nothing, while those living in the cold north wore layers of hides and furs. People who had to spend all their time looking for food didn't have much time for making fancy or beautiful things to wear. Those who had plenty of food had the time to create intricate jewelry and clothing with elaborate decorations made from quills, shells, beads, paints, and embroidery.

Tribes in the central Plains area usually wore clothing made of hides because they hunted large animals like elk and buffalo that lived there. Those living in the warm grasslands of California wove their simple clothing from grass and went barefoot.

Many Indian people enjoyed wearing all their jewelry when they could. It showed off their wealth and they believed that certain types of decoration gave them good luck or strength.

Because Native American people wore clothing that was made from whatever they could hunt or gather, there is no one certain style of clothing that was worn by all tribes. Some wore grass skirts; others wore clothes woven from strips of bark. Some wore nothing at all!

The clothing we see most often is that of the Plains people. They dressed entirely in hides. They cleaned and tanned buffalo hides and deerskin until they were soft and flexible. They painted or sewed on decorations like beads, quills, bells, shells, stones, and even horsehair and feathers.

No matter what materials Indian people found, they tried to use them to dress in an elegant and beautiful way.

> ***Good Idea*** *While sewing hides, some Indian women used thorns from trees to hold the pieces together in the same way sewing pins are used today.*

Paper Bag Vest

The Blackfoot, Chippewa, Sioux, and Crow people made vests from animal hides or fabric they traded for. Vests were useful, easy to make, and beautifully decorated. The Plains tribes used mostly geometric designs for decoration. The Eastern tribes, like the Chippewas, decorated with floral designs that were simple and brightly colored. Decorate yours however you choose.

Fast Fact *Hide clothing was made from the skin of antelope, moose, elk, caribou, buffalo or deer. Deerskin was the finest and most desired because it was soft and lightly colored. To make the skin soft, the hair was scraped off and the hide was soaked in water and animal brains. Then it was pounded, stretched, and smoked over a campfire.*

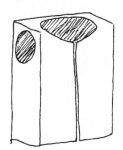

Cut arm and neck openings.

Staple at the shoulders for reinforcement.

Decorate with crayons or markers.

Reinforce with a piece of tape before punching holes for ties.

MATERIALS

Large brown paper bag
Yarn
Scissors
Stapler
Paints or colored markers
Tape
Hole punch

 Cut the front and neck opening from the bag. Cut out 2 circles at the sides for arm openings. Pull up the shoulders and staple them securely for reinforcement. You may need to trim off some of the bottom of the bag if it is too long.

Decorate the bag with geometric or floral designs as you like. You can also cut a fringe along the bottom edge.

To add a tie at the neck, reinforce both of the front neck edges with tape, and then punch 2 holes and thread a piece of yarn through.

Breechcloth and Apron

MATERIALS

Plains style:
Cloth, 1 by 4 feet
Belt

Woodland style:
Large brown paper bag
Yarn
Paint or markers
Hole punch
Wide masking tape

Woodland people wore aprons that tied at the sides.

The Plains Indians wore breechcloths made of buckskin or cloth about 12 inches wide and 6 feet long. They were draped in front and back over a belt at the waist. They were worn by boys and men, and tribes made them in different styles and from various materials. You can make one by wrapping a long piece of fabric (1 foot wide and 4 feet long) through a belt at your waist.

The Woodland Indian people wore an apron instead of a breechcloth. To make one like theirs, cut the sides from a large brown paper grocery sack. Decorate the 2 sections with paint or markers. The Woodland people used designs with flowers and curving leaves. Reinforce the waist with wide masking tape. Punch holes and tie at the sides with pieces of colored yarn.

If you have a sewing machine, you can stitch colorful bias seam binding across the top of the front and back sections, leaving lengths at the ends for tying. Ask a grown-up to help you with the machine.

Wrap the breechcloth over a belt at the waist.

Tie on over a pair of jeans.

Leggings

MATERIALS

Old pair of jeans
2 leather bootlaces or
sturdy cord for tying
Felt
Scraps of white felt, or
a plastic bottle (optional)
Scissors
Acrylic paint
Glue
Hole punch

 For a boy's leggings, cut the jeans as shown. Girls' leggings only covered the calf of their leg, from the ankle to the knee.

Cut away the front and back of the jeans, leaving belt loops at the side so that a boy can wear them with a belt. Of course, swim trunks and a breechcloth will be needed, too!

For a girl, cut the leg sections of the jeans off below the knee. Cut slits along the top of the girl's leggings and lace the bootlaces through. They will be tied in place above the calf.

Decorate the leggings with acrylic paints or geometric shapes cut from felt and glued in place. Cut strips of felt into fringe and glue it down the side, too. Some Indians used concho shells to decorate their leggings and clothing. You can make your conchos by cutting circles from white felt or a white plastic bottle. Punch 2 holes in the center and lace through the jean fabric with lengths of yarn. Knot them securely.

> **Good Idea** Indians traded for sewing thread when the traders arrived. However, before that they used "sinew." Sinew is a long muscle from the back of an elk or deer. It is stringy and can be pulled apart in thin threads. Thin pieces of sinew and bone needles were used to sew tiny bone beads and porcupine quills to clothing for decoration.

Many tribes wore leggings. Men and boys wore them to cover their legs completely. Women and girls wore shorter ones that went from the ankle to just below the knee. Leggings kept their legs warm and protected them from scratchy bushes, insects, and snakes.

Leggings were made from soft deerskin and decorated with beads and fringe. Men's leggings tied onto a belt at the waist; women's tied just below the knee. Men wore breechcloths with theirs; women wore dresses over them. Children usually dressed just like their parents.

> **Fast Fact** Bone needles have been found in Washington state that are over 10,000 years old.

For boys: Cut away the front and back of the jeans. Leave a belt loop on each side so that you can wear them with a belt.

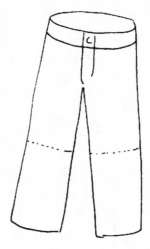

Cut off lower legs to use for girls' leggings.

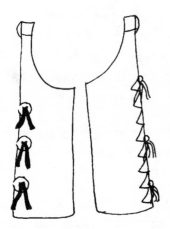

Decorate with felt pieces, yarn tassels, and conchos made from felt or plastic bottles.

Girls tie theirs at the top. Cut a strip of felt fringe and glue down the side.

Armbands

MATERIALS

Narrow, round plastic bottle
(shampoo or
liquid detergent bottle)
Colored cloth or felt (optional)
Yarn or leather shoelace
Paper tube from gift wrap or
paper towels
Aluminum foil
Scissors
Hole punch
Markers or crayons

Cut an armband shape from the upper rounded portion of the plastic bottle. Use scissors and trim the edges so that they are rounded. Decorate with designs made by punching holes in the plastic. Draw designs on the plastic with a permanent marker.

Add a medallion by cutting a circle from a flat part of the bottle or from colored cloth or felt. Punch 2 holes in the medallion and in the side of the armband. Thread it in place with a piece of yarn or leather shoelace.

You can use paper tubes to make armbands that you color with markers or crayons. Wrap and glue on aluminum foil to make the tubes look like the silver jewelry worn by the people of the Southwest.

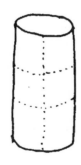

Cut armbands from paper tubes.

Trim the corners to round the edges.

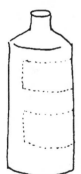

Cut armbands from plastic bottles.

Color with markers or punch holes and tie on a shell gorget cut from a flat section of the bottle.

45

Cuffs

Decorated bands were worn on the wrist or arm. They weren't practical for daily work or hunting, but were worn for ceremonies, feasts, and dances.

Sioux, Ute, Crow, and Cheyenne people made cuffs of hide and decorated them with beads and fringe.

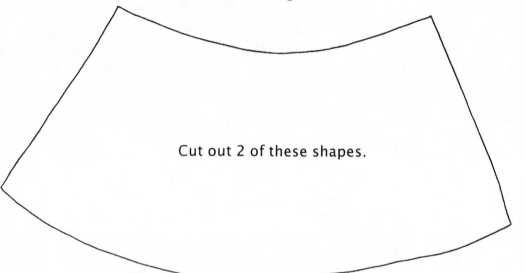

Cut out 2 of these shapes.

✿ Make your own cuffs by cutting the shape shown from vinyl, heavy fabric, or construction paper. Decorate with paint or colored markers. Cut a strip of paper fringe, and staple or glue it in place along 1 side. Staple the 2 pieces together at the sides. Slip the cuffs over your hands.

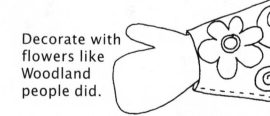

Decorate with flowers like Woodland people did.

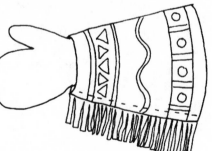

Use geometric designs like the Plains people. Staple on a strip of fringe.

Anklets

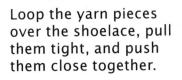

Loop the yarn pieces over the shoelace, pull them tight, and push them close together.

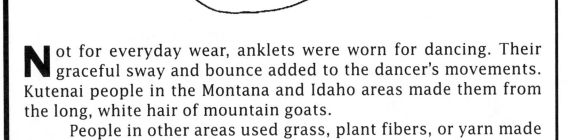

MATERIALS

White yarn
2 shoelaces
Bells (optional)
Scissors

Cut the yarn into 8-inch pieces. Loop and knot them onto the shoelace. Continue adding yarn until you have enough to wrap around your ankle. Tie the shoelace at the back of your leg and arrange the yarn fringe so that it hides the shoelace. As your legs move, the yarns will ripple and bounce. You can also tie on a tinkling bell to add a jingling sound.

Not for everyday wear, anklets were worn for dancing. Their graceful sway and bounce added to the dancer's movements. Kutenai people in the Montana and Idaho areas made them from the long, white hair of mountain goats.

   People in other areas used grass, plant fibers, or yarn made from sheep's wool.

Fancy Dance Bustle

MATERIALS

Round pizza cardboard or
cardboard cut in a circle
Narrow belt or fabric sash
Construction paper
in various colors
Scissors
Glue

Cut 2 slits in the card-
board to thread the belt or
fabric sash through.

Cut several construction
paper feathers, using one as a
pattern.

Glue the feathers over the
cardboard in a circular pattern,
starting at the outer edge.
Layer a row of shorter ones at
the center.

Tie the bustle on so that it
fits snugly on your back, and
you're ready to dance to the
drumming! You can make 2
smaller bustles with small
paper plates to tie onto your
upper arms.

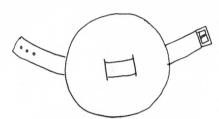

Cut 2 slits to slide the
belt through.

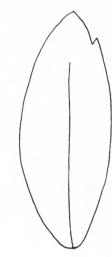

Cut several
paper feathers
and glue over
the cardboard.

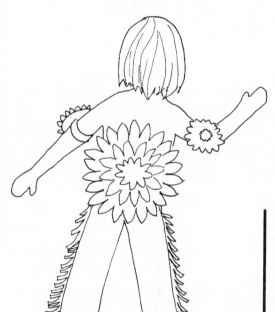

Indian dancers today wear
elaborate rainbow-colored
fancy dance bustles on their
backs. They are made from
feathers layered in a pattern
over a round base. Smaller
bustles are tied onto the
dancer's upper arm.

Women and Girls' Cape

20 to 24 inches

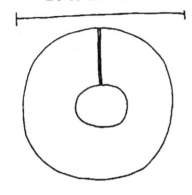

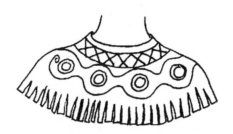

MATERIALS

Large, heavy paper
(shelf paper, butcher paper,
or newspaper)
Large safety pin
Scissors
Markers or crayons

Some design ideas

Cut a circle about 20 inches in diameter, depending upon the size of your neck. Cut a front opening and neck area. Cut a fringe around the outside edge of the cape.

Decorate your cape with markers or crayons. Pin it at the back of the neck with the safety pin when you wear it.

Women and girls in the Great Lakes area wore short leather capes over their dresses. They decorated them with designs made with porcupine quills or tiny beads.

Pueblo Dress

MATERIALS

2 bath towels
2 large safety pins
Long fabric sash or
rope for belt
Sewing machine

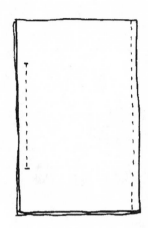

Sew 2 bath towels together like this.

Ask a grown-up to sew the towels together as shown. Pin at the shoulder. Wrap the sash around your waist and tie it.

Hopi girls wore thick leggings made by winding wide strips of white fabric around their legs. You can tear an old bedsheet into strips and wrap them around your legs from the ankles to the knees. Tuck the ends inside the wrapping.

Fold one side under your arm. Pin the other at the shoulder. Wrap a sash at the waist.

Hopi women of the Southwest wove colorful fabric on looms. They made it from the cotton they grew. Later, they began using wool from their sheep. They made the fabric into simple dresses that left one shoulder bare and were belted with a sash at the waist. Older women wore shawls over their heads and shoulders.

Headbands

Headbands were worn by many different tribes. Make yours as unique as you are by decorating with geometric or floral designs, or whatever strikes your fancy.

MATERIALS

Heavy paper (colored paper, tagboard, or strips of wallpaper)

Construction paper in various colors

Markers or crayons

Scissors

Stapler or heavy tape

Glue on paper shells and feathers.

Cut feathers from paper and staple them to the band. Staple or tape the ends of the band together to fit your head.

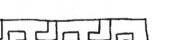

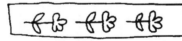

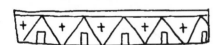

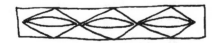

Make patterns of shapes or flowers for your band.

Fast Fact In some tribes the men grew very long hair. A Crow chief named Long Hair had hair that measured 10 feet and 7 inches long. He wrapped it around a piece of wood that he carried under his arm. Some tribes even tried to make their hair appear longer by gluing on extra hair.

Warbonnets

Today, soldiers earn medals and ribbons for acts of bravery in the military. Indian warriors earned eagle feathers that they displayed on headbands. Warbonnets were treasured and worn by men who had earned the right to wear each feather by doing a brave deed. A council would listen to the man tell about the experience, and then decide if he deserved the honor of wearing the feather.

If a man won more honor feathers then he could fit on the band around his head, he could add rows of feathers hanging down his back. Some men won so many honors that their bonnets dragged on the ground, so they put the extra feathers on a lance or pole for display.

Eagle feathers were used because they were hard to get and because the eagle was a powerful bird. The wearer hoped he might get some of the eagle's power from the feathers.

You can make different styles of warbonnets. The Blackfoot bonnet has all the feathers sticking up around the headband. The Apache bonnet is a cap with feathers that droops over the head all around. Western Plains tribes wore bonnets that went over the back, sometimes reaching the ankles.

Blackfoot Bonnet

Color the feather tips dark brown, like eagle feathers.

MATERIALS

Tagboard strip, 3 inches wide and long enough to fit around your head, plus 2 inches
White paper
Cotton balls
Markers or crayons
Stapler
Scissors
Glue

Staple or glue feathers all around the headband. Glue cotton balls at the base of each feather.

Color and decorate the tagboard headband strip with markers or crayons. Blackfoot people liked to use geometric designs, so use lots of zigzags, triangles, and straight lines. Adjust it to fit your head and staple it, over-lapping the ends.

Make a feather shape to use as a pattern. Trace around it to make several feathers. Use a dark brown crayon or marker to draw lines down the center and color the tip of the feather.

Staple or glue the feathers in place around the headband. Indians used the tiny white plume feathers that grow in an eagle's tail as fluffs for decoration. To make fluffs for your headband, glue a white cotton ball at the base of each paper feather.

Apache Bonnet

Glue paper feathers around the coffee filter.

Use hairpins to hold it in place on top of your head.

MATERIALS

White paper
Large paper coffee filter
Hairpins
Pencil
Scissors
Markers or crayons
Glue or stapler

 Draw and cut out a feather to use as a pattern. Trace and cut out several feathers from white paper. Use a dark brown crayon or marker to color the tip and center of each feather so that they look like eagle feathers.

Glue or staple them in place around the edge of the coffee filter. They should stick out and be floppy. This type of bonnet needs a couple of hairpins to pin it in place towards the back of your head so that the feathers aren't in your eyes.

MATERIALS

Large brown paper bag
Tagboard strip, 2 inches wide
and long enough to fit around
your head, plus 2 inches
Scissors
Pencil
Crayons or markers
Stapler

Cut the bottom out of the bag. Fold it in half lengthwise twice and cut it in half as shown. Draw and cut out 2 feather shapes and a headband in 1 piece as shown. Repeat for the other section of the folded bag. Unfold. Color the feathers with crayons or markers.

Staple the tagboard headband to fit your head. Staple 1 strip of feathers to the headband. Cut the other section of feathers in half to make 2 equal sections. Staple them to the sides of the headband so that they drape down your back.

Plains Bonnet

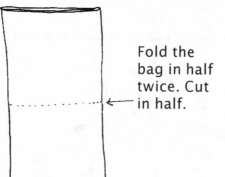

Fold the bag in half twice. Cut in half.

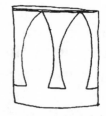

Draw and cut out both pieces like this.

Some tribes added buffalo horns to their bonnet. Cut 2 curved shapes from colored paper and staple them at the sides.

Tape on an additional feather whenever you accomplish a brave or noble deed!

Staple one piece over the headband. Staple the other pieces to the sides so that they drop down your back.

Bonnet Case

Warriors were careful to store their prized bonnets in cases made from stiff hide. Make one for your bonnet.

MATERIALS

Oatmeal box
Construction paper
2 pieces of yarn or leather bootlaces, 12 inches long
Markers or paint
Scissors
Hole punch

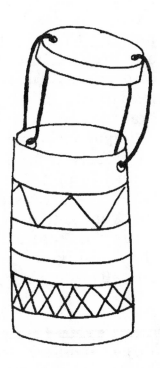

Cover the oatmeal box with construction paper. Draw designs or paint on it to make it special. Use a hole punch to make holes in the lid and sides. Thread the yarn or bootlaces through the holes and tie the ends in a knot.

To put your bonnet inside, roll it up and put the headband side in first.

Iroquois Headdress

MATERIALS

Construction paper
White paper
Cotton balls
Scissors
Markers or crayons
Stapler
Pencil
Glue

Cut the construction paper into 3 strips: make one 20 by 2 inches and two that are 12 by 2 inches. Decorate 1 side of the longer strip. The Iroquois were a Woodland tribe and they liked to use flower designs in bright colors, usually with a black or dark blue background.

Staple the long strip to make a headband to fit your head. Staple the 2 smaller strips to the headband, crossing as shown.

Cut several small paper feather shapes from the white paper and staple them to the cap frame. Draw and cut 1 large feather. Staple it to

the top center and bend it so that it sticks up a bit.

Indians would have used the delicate, fluffy, white plumes from an eagle's tail for the very top. You can glue a ring of cotton balls around the base of the large feather.

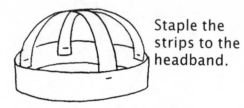

Staple the strips to the headband.

Cover the cap with paper feathers. Make a larger one to stick up at the top. Glue cotton balls around it for plumes.

Indians who lived in the open plains and deserts could wear the long, flowing feathered bonnets without much trouble, but the tribes that lived in forested or heavily wooded areas had problems moving through the bushes and trees without snagging and losing their precious feathers on overhanging branches.

Iroquois men made caps that fit closely to their heads for displaying their feathers. When they traveled through the woods, they removed the large top feathers and put them back on when they arrived at their destination.

Good Manners *Indian men didn't shave, they removed their whiskers by pulling each one out with tweezers made of bone or shell.*

Pipe Bone Breastplate

People living in the Plains and Plateau areas wore breastplates for decoration. They were first made from the narrow dentalium shells traded from the coast tribes. Later they were made from buffalo and cow bones and were called "pipe bones." Settlers made them to trade with the Indians, too.

Men's breastplates came to the waist. Some women and girls were wealthy enough to have breastplates that hung to the ground. They were trimmed with bells and jinglers and were very heavy.

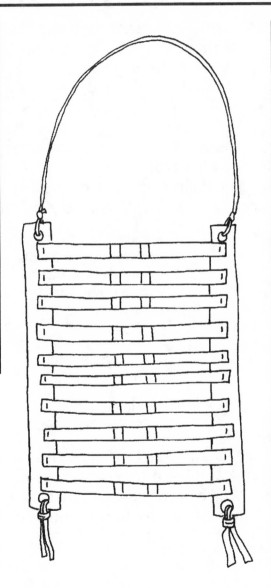

MATERIALS

White tagboard or posterboard
Yarn
Scissors
Stapler
Hole punch
Colored markers

Cut 2 side strips from the tagboard that are 10 by 1 inches, and cut 10 more strips 8 by ½ inches.

Staple the narrow strips to the 2 wider ones at the sides, spacing the strips about ½ inch apart.

Punch a hole at the top of the side strips and tie on enough yarn to go around your neck.

Cut two 6-inch pieces of yarn. Punch a hole at the bottom of the side strips, loop the yarn through the hole, and knot it to hang as a tassel.

Use markers to color the center sections of the strips to look like colored beads and bone sections.

Bear Claw Necklace

MATERIALS

Plastic Claws
White plastic bottle
Hole punch
Brown marker

Salt Dough Claws
4 cups flour
1½ cups water
1 cup salt
Skewer, chopstick, or nail
Brown paint
Acrylic finish,
acrylic floor wax,
or clear nail polish (optional)
Yarn or cord
Macaroni
Drinking straws
Fake fur, fabric, or cotton balls
Scissors
Glue

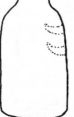 Cut claw shapes from the plastic bottle, using the curving sides to get a curved shape like real claws. Punch holes in the tops. Color them brown.

To make the salt dough claws, mix the flour, water, and salt together and knead it about 5 minutes until the dough is soft and pliable. Shape it into claws. Poke the skewer, chopstick, or nail through the ends to make holes for stringing. Bake at 250°F until they are hard.

Let them cool, and then paint them brown. To make them shiny, coat with acrylic finish, acrylic floor wax, or clear nail polish.

Cut claws from a plastic bottle. Punch a hole in the end. Color dark brown with a permanent marker.

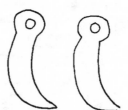

Shape claws from dough. Make a hole in the end before baking.

A man was very lucky if he survived a fight with a grizzly bear and lived to wear its claws as a necklace!

You can make your own bear claws out of plastic bottles or homemade clay to wear on a necklace.

String your claws onto a piece of yarn or cord, spacing them apart with 3 pieces of macaroni between each. You can use short pieces cut from drinking straws, too.

Small rectangles of fake fur can be strung between the claws. Cut shapes from fake fur fabric, fold the pieces in half, and glue together over the necklace cord.

When you are finished, knot the ends together.

Fast Fact *Tribes had different hairstyles. Pawnee men shaved their whole heads. Crow and Sioux men rubbed bear grease in theirs and grew it as long as they could. Hopi girls wore their hair in twists over their ears until they married. They wore one long braid after the marriage.*

String macaroni between the claws.

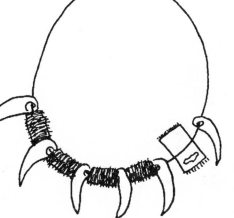

Glue fake fur or fabric or gently stretch and glue cotton balls around the string between the claws.

Use some of the dough to make beads for other projects.

Shell Necklace

MATERIALS

Macaroni,
shell- and tube-shaped
Water
Food coloring (optional)
Aluminum foil
(recycle an old piece, and
add it to your recycling bin
when you are finished)
Heavy-duty sewing thread
or yarn
Small bowl
Large nail

Fill the bowl halfway with water. If you want colored shells, add a few drops of food coloring to the water to tint it. Drop in a handful of uncooked macaroni shells. Let them soak until they soften enough to poke a nail through. Poke a hole in each shell. Lay the wet shells on aluminum foil to dry. Make sure the shells don't touch each other or they will be stuck together.

When the shells are dry, string them on the thread. Put pieces of tube-shaped macaroni between the shells as spacers.

You might want to use other things with your shells, like pieces of cut-up drinking straws, Styrofoam packing pellets (string them with a threaded darning needle), circles cut from felt, leather or fake fur, buttons, or plastic bottle caps (poke holes in them with a nail).

Poke holes in
soft pasta shells
with a nail.

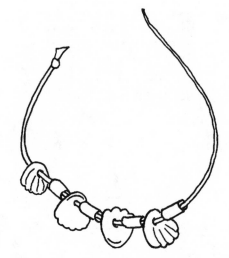

Pasta or cut-up
drinking straws.

Shell Gorget

These pendants were worn by Indians in the Southeastern part of the United States. They are known for the large mounds they built by piling earth and rocks into unusual shapes. Some mounds are shaped like huge serpents and are over 20 feet wide and a quarter mile long! The earth is still piled in the unusual shapes, even after 2,000 years. In other places, up to 100 mounds were built together; another huge pyramid mound is almost as large as the Great Pyramid in Egypt. We don't know exactly why they built them, but they were probably part of their religion or were burial sites.

These Mound Builders also carved shapes from shells using tools made from bone or stone, and wore them on cords around their necks.

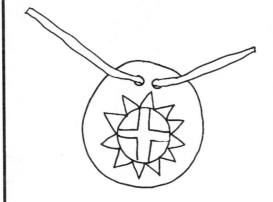

MATERIALS

Styrofoam plate or meat tray
Tissue
Yarn, 24 inches long
White air-dry clay or home-made salt dough (optional)
Clear nail polish (optional)
Scissors
Ballpoint pen or sharp pencil
Water-based marker
Toothpick

 Cut a round shape from Styrofoam. Poke 2 holes through it for threading with yarn.

Draw a few designs on paper first, and then press the design into the Styrofoam with a ballpoint pen or pencil.

To make the design show up, color over it with a water-based marker. Wipe it with a tissue, letting the color settle into the design grooves.

String your pendant onto the yarn, tie it, and wear it to bring you luck and skill, as the Indians did.

You can also make a pendant out of clay. Use white air-dry clay or make homemade salt dough.

Simple Salt Dough: Mix 4 parts of flour with 1 part of salt. Stir in just enough warm water to moisten. Knead until it's soft and workable. Keep it in a plastic bag, taking out only enough to work with so it won't dry out.

Use a toothpick to draw designs and press holes for the yarn to go through. When it's dry and hard, brush on clear nail polish and string it on yarn.

Shell Etching

 Paint a design on the shell with the nail polish. Use a simple geometric design. If you want to use a brush with a fine tip to make a very delicate design, be sure to clean the brush with polish remover before the polish dries and makes the bristles hard.

After the polish dries, soak the shell in a small bowl of vinegar for 24 hours.

Rinse it off. Drill a hole in the end to hang from a necklace or use a hot glue gun to attach the shell to old jewelry to make a pin, barrette, or bolo tie. You can also attach it to a refrigerator magnet if you wish.

MATERIALS

Clam shell
(in the seafood section of the grocery store,
or ask a restaurant to save some for you)
Clear nail polish and remover
Vinegar
Fine-tipped brush (optional)
Small bowl or mug
Drill or hot glue gun
(for grown-up use)

Ancient Hohokam people lived in the desert in Arizona. They made unusual jewelry by etching designs on shells. They probably used cactus juice to eat away the shell's surface and leave a design. You can try a similar process yourself.

Paint a design with nail polish.

Soak in vinegar.

Glue the shell to jewelry backings to make bolo ties, hair barrettes, or pins.

Fetish Necklace

A fetish is an object thought to have a magical power. It brings good luck and power to the owner. Indian fetishes were usually in the shape of animals and other living things and were treated carefully. A fetish was worn around the neck like a necklace, carried in a special bag, or tied to a horse's reins. They were even attached to babies' cradleboards.

The Hidatsa people, who valued women who worked hard, tied the teeth of a beaver around a little girl's neck, hoping it would make her a good worker.

The first fetishes were stones that had the shape of particular animals. The Indians carved them with stone tools to make them look more like real animals. They told stories about how these unusual stones were animals or people who had turned to stone.

Today, the Zuni artists of the Southwest carve tiny birds and animals from unusual stones or shells. They string them with beads to create beautiful necklaces.

You can carve a fetish from a bar of soap, using a spoon, vegetable peeler, or a table knife. When you have finished carving, wet your hands with water and smooth over the surface. Use the simple shape of a bear, which Indians felt to be a powerful fetish. Tie a string around its middle to hold a feather, pretty bead, or paper arrowhead to its back.

You can also shape fetishes from salt dough or self-hardening clay. Poke holes with a toothpick for stringing if you want to wear them around your neck.

Make a necklace with many fetishes. Cut small bird and animal shapes from posterboard, thin Styrofoam, or flat plastic bottles.

Poke or punch holes for stringing.

Carve the soap with a spoon, vegetable peeler, or knife. Smooth with water.

Make a bear shape.

Tie a bead and paper arrowhead to its back.

Navajos wore tiny skin bags on thongs around their necks. It held tiny fetishes and the remains of their own umbilical cord—a valued possession.

 Make a felt bag by folding a rectangle of felt in half and gluing it at the sides. String it onto a piece of yarn. Make an animal fetish from an animal cracker cookie. Wind a piece of yarn around its back and knot a tiny bead on it. Carry your special good luck charm in the bag.

Good Idea *Beaver teeth were used as knives to carve antler, bone, wood, or soft stone.*
Native Wisdom *Belief in the spirits helped people explain the unknown.*

Wrap yarn around a cookie. Store it in the bag.

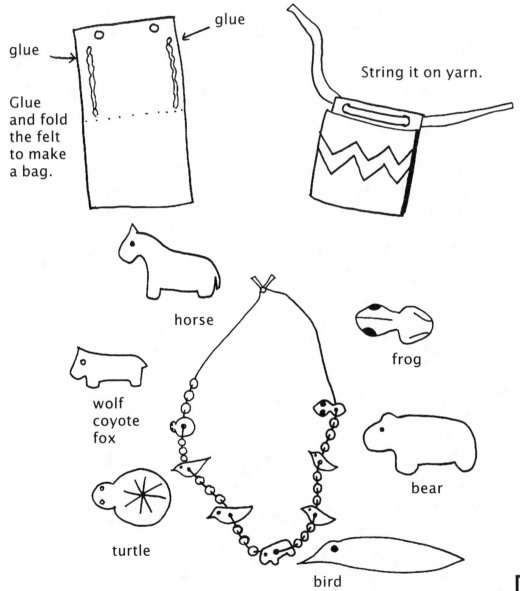

glue

glue

Glue and fold the felt to make a bag.

String it on yarn.

horse

wolf
coyote
fox

turtle

frog

bear

bird

Seed and Corn Necklace

To make a seed necklace, save and wash seeds from squash, watermelons, sunflowers, and corn. To get colored corn, buy decorative "Indian corn" and rub the kernels off the cob. **WARNING:** Don't use packages of seed corn—they are treated with poison and may make you sick. Use dried beans or small peanuts in the shell—whatever you can find to string.

Soak the seeds, beans, or corn kernels in a bowl of water until they are soft enough to poke the needle through. It will take a few hours or overnight, depending upon the beans you are using.

Thread the needle with a double length of thread long enough to create the necklace you want. Knot the thread end around the first kernel on the string. It will secure it so that the kernels and seeds don't slide off as you string them. When the necklace is finished, knot the ends together securely.

MATERIALS

Dried seeds, beans, and corn kernels
Heavy thread
Water
Bowl
Darning needle

Before Indians began trading with Europeans for small glass beads, they made jewelry out of seeds, shells, stones, bird talons, and animal teeth and claws. They used what they found around them or what they had traded with other tribes.

Silver Bracelet

Indians in the Southwest are known for their beautiful silver work. For centuries, they have made jewelry from turquoise stones, clay beads, shells, and wood. When the Spaniards arrived, the Indians began trading with them for Spanish silver coins. At first they hammered the coins into shapes, but later they learned from Mexican craftsmen how to cast shapes in melted silver. The Hopi, Navajo, and Zuni tribes of the Southwest make most of the silver jewelry that is sold today.

You can make a bracelet quickly and easily that looks like silver jewelry made in the Southwest.

MATERIALS

Narrow, round plastic bottles
(shampoo or liquid
detergent bottles)
Aluminum foil
Scissors
Glue

✿✿ Cut a bracelet shape from the bottle. Make it as wide or narrow as you want. You can cut 3 or 4 from 1 shampoo bottle. Trim the ends so that they curve, or leave them in circles if they are wide enough for you to slide your hand through to make a bracelet.

Tear a piece of aluminum foil large enough to wrap around the bracelet. Wrap and glue it in place over the plastic with the shiny side out. Smooth out all the wrinkles with your fingertips.

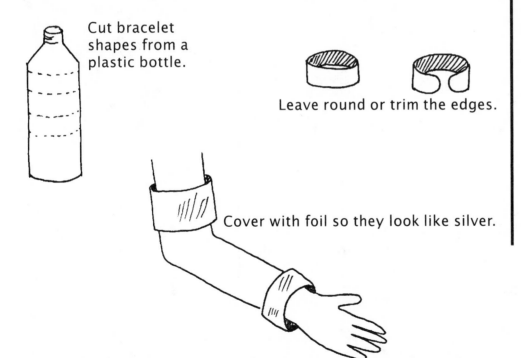

Cut bracelet shapes from a plastic bottle.

Leave round or trim the edges.

Cover with foil so they look like silver.

Earring Loops

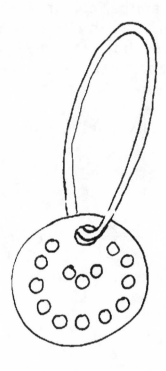

MATERIALS

2 plastic milk bottle caps
Yarn
Nail or hole punch
Permanent markers

Earrings were not widely popular with North American Indians. Usually men wore them, and they were made of shells or stones.

Make a pair to hang from loops over your ears.

Punch a hole in the tops of both lids. Draw designs on the lid with the markers. Thread a piece of yarn through the hole and knot the ends.

To wear, hang them over your ears and let them dangle.

PLAY CLAY

1 cup flour
1 tablespoon salad oil
1 cup water
½ cup salt
2 teaspoons cream of tartar
Food coloring

It's fun to make beads from clay or homemade clay dough. Here's a recipe that dries hard without baking.

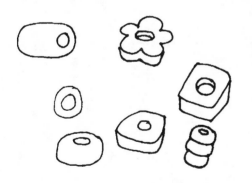

Use a nail to poke holes for stringing.

Homemade Clay Beads

Indians put beads on everything—belts, clothing, shoes, horse gear, tepees, cradleboards, and, of course, around their necks!

Beads were made from whatever materials people could find or trade for. Shells, fish and animal bones, pebbles, claws, nuts, seeds, porcupine quills, dried berries, deer horns, metal pieces, hardened clay, birds' claws—all were used as beads. Holes were made with stone tools. In later years, they traded with fur traders for glass beads made in Europe.

"Pony" beads were one-color glass beads that they took west on pony pack trains for trading. "Seed" beads are the tiny beads Indians sewed onto clothing to create fancy designs.

You can make beads from macaroni, clay, paper, or cut-up drinking straws.

Combine everything in a large saucepan. Stir constantly over medium heat. It will thicken slowly and then become a big ball. Spoon the dough onto a floured surface and knead when cool.

Shape into beads. Use nails, coffee stirrers, drinking straws, pencils, or chopsticks to punch holes for stringing. Let them dry until they are hard. Decorate them with paint or permanent markers if you want.

Paper Beads

Cut triangles or rectangles from paper. Roll them around a pencil and glue the end in place. String them on a piece of yarn when the glue is dry.

Use colorful papers cut from magazines or gift wrap, or use pieces of aluminum foil to make beads that look like silver.

Make easy paper beads by crushing balls of colored tissue paper and stringing them with a needle and thread. You can string cotton balls, cut-up drinking straws, and dry pasta, too.

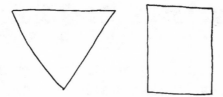

Cut paper shapes.

Roll up and tape or glue the ends.

String crushed balls of colored tissue paper, cotton balls, cut-up drinking straws, and dry pasta.

Face Painting

Indians painted their faces and bodies for many reasons. They painted their bodies with designs to protect them before they went to war. They painted their faces to be more attractive, just as women do nowadays. They used paint to protect their skin from sun and wind, just as we use sunscreen today. Paint also kept flies, mosquitoes, and other annoying insects away, just like insect repellent.

Sometimes people painted their faces to show that they belonged to a club or society. Faces were painted for ceremonies and to mourn someone who died.

Indians made the paints they used out of certain clays, charcoal, berries, and moss that they ground up. They used stones to grind the materials into powder, and then mixed the powder with animal fat.

A good sunscreen was made by rubbing buffalo fat on the face, spreading powdered paint over it, and rubbing it in.

Men in an Omaha war party painted their faces with streaks running down from their eyes to show that they were crying for the success of their expedition.

Pawnee scouts painted their faces white to symbolize the wolf, whose power was thought to be of great help when scouting.

A Sioux would show others he wanted to be left alone or had fallen in love by painting his face black and then using his fingernails to scrape a zigzag from hairline to chin.

Sioux women who wanted to be beautiful would paint a red streak from ear to ear across their face and add a red streak of paint down the part in their hair.

When an Arikara girl was in love, she painted her cheeks with dots.

Colors of paint meant certain things. Most of the tribes used colors to mean these things:

black = death
red = power and life
blue = sky
yellow = joy and victory
white = peace

Go ahead and experiment with face painting. Use theatrical face makeup or paint especially for face painting. Follow the directions on the package.

> **Depending on Plants** *Walnut hulls were rubbed on gray hair to make it dark again.*

Masks

Indians believed there were many spirits. To please these spirits, some tribes made masks to wear during special dances and ceremonies. Some tribes wore masks and special costumes during ceremonies to teach or remind people about their religion and history.

Masks were made many different ways. The simplest mask was made from the head of a large animal, like a buffalo, bear, or deer. The Iroquois and the Northwest Coast tribes carved wood into masks. Some tribes wove masks from grass or corn husks. People made masks from the materials they found around them, depending on the land and climate of their homes.

Mudhead Mask

In the Southwest, clowns were part of some Zuni ceremonies. They acted silly and funny, trying to make the audience laugh. The Zuni called them Koyemshi, and sometimes "Mudheads."

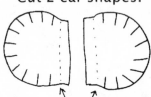

Cut 2 ear shapes.

Fold on broken lines.

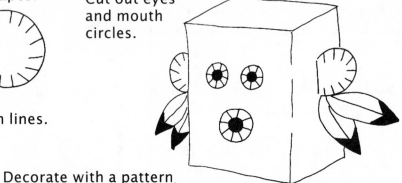

Cut out eyes and mouth circles.

Decorate with a pattern of straight lines.

MATERIALS

Large brown paper bag
Construction paper
Scissors
Pencil
Black marker
Glue
Stapler

Trim a bit off the bottom of the bag so that it fits you. It should rest on your head and just touch the tops of your shoulders.

Cut 2 paper ears. Fold them along an edge and glue them in place at the sides of the bag. Try on the bag, and locate spots to cut out holes for your eyes and mouth. Lay the bag down on a flat surface, draw circles for eye and mouth holes, and cut them out. Draw circle and line patterns around the cutout area.

Draw and cut out 4 paper feathers. Staple them to the bottom of each ear.

MATERIALS

Cereal box
Red or black paint (or both)
Black yarn
Narrow elastic braid
Scissors
Stapler
Hole punch

Cut the box apart and use the front or back panel. Cut 2 slits 3 inches long at the top corners. Overlap and staple them. Trim the bottom corners away as shown. Cut out 2 eye holes. Paint the mask red, black, or both colors, trying to make it ugly and scary.

Punch holes around the top and sides and tie on yarn hair. Punch 2 holes at the sides and tie on a piece of elastic, adjusting it to fit your head.

False Face Mask

Iroquois people tried to scare away evil and sickness by wearing ugly masks. They carved them from wood and tied clumps of horsehair to them.

The color the masks were painted depended upon when they were made. If the mask was carved before noon, it was painted black. If it was made after noon, it was painted red. If it was worked on in both the morning and afternoon, it was painted red and black. Keep this in mind when you decide to make yours so that you can paint it the correct color!

Cut two 3-inch slits.

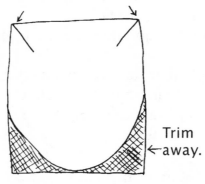

Trim
←away.

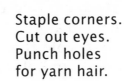

Staple corners.
Cut out eyes.
Punch holes
for yarn hair.

Decorate to
make it very
scary!

73

Kachina Mask

The Hopi people of the Southwest believed that Kachinas were spirits that lived in the mountains and visited their villages. There were over 200 different Kachinas. Adults made small dolls to help the children learn all of them. Some Kachina spirits were helpful and kind; some were not. Men dressed as Kachinas for special religious dances.

Make a Kachina mask for yourself.

 Cut the tube to make a nose that is about 3 inches long. Cover it with a strip of colored paper and glue it in place. Cut ½-inch slits at one end to make tabs. Fold the tabs toward the inside of the tube, put glue on them, and attach the tube to the mask.

Cut 2 paper ear shapes. Fold them along 1 edge and glue them to the sides of the mask. Cut out holes for eyes.

Cut the crepe paper in 4-inch strips. Staple it around the neck edge of the carton to make a ruff. Pleat it at each staple to make it full. Cut a long strip of paper and glue it on so that it covers the staples.

Cut out and glue on paper feathers here and there.

MATERIALS

Round cardboard ice cream carton
(Try to get the large kind from an ice cream store.
If you use a gallon container, make a cut up the back and across the top so that you can fit your head inside it.)
Paper tube from toilet tissue or paper towel roll
Colored construction paper
Crepe paper
Scissors
Glue
Stapler

Make a nose by cutting, folding, and gluing a paper tube.

Cut 2 ear shapes.

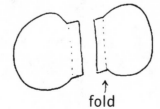

fold

74

SONG AND DANCE

Songs were very important to all Native American people. They were learned and passed on to the next generation to sing in worship, for thanks, or during celebration. Most songs were part of their religion.

Plains people owned the songs they made up. Unless they were sold or inherited, no one else could sing these songs. Each person had his or her own special song. They believed that a person had no power without his or her song. Warriors sang their songs in battle. They also had death songs to sing if they were captured by enemies.

Dances were part of their religion, too. There were special dances for different ceremonies. Sometimes a dance was for only men or only women; sometimes a dance was for everyone.

Some dances were to cure illness, and they were sometimes wild and scary as the dancers tried to scare away the evil that they thought was causing the sickness.

Dancers often wore special costumes and masks to represent spirits or animals.

During a dance, people would sing or chant, and musicians would play drums, rattles, or other instruments. Dances often lasted for hours, sometimes days, when they were part of a special ceremony.

Native Americans didn't dance for fun and entertainment. Their dances were like prayers. They danced to ask the gods for things, to request good luck in hunting, or to celebrate gifts from nature.

They danced before battles for luck and afterwards to celebrate victory.

Fast Fact *Flutes were made and used by young men to serenade their sweethearts.*

Musical Rasp

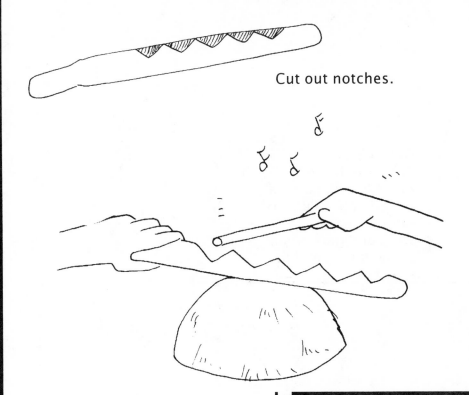

Cut out notches.

MATERIALS

Paint stirring stick,
1½ by 12 inches
(free in paint stores) or
a wooden ruler
12-by-½-inch stick,
an unsharpened pencil,
or a dowel
Small handsaw
Half a coconut shell or
a clean plastic margarine tub

✿ Cut notches in the thicker stick using the saw. Ask a grown-up to help you with this part. Make several notches about an inch apart.

To play music, place the coconut shell or margarine tub flat on the ground. Hold the notched stick by one end and place it against the shell. Strum it by dragging the stick back and forth over the notches.

T he Basin-Plateau tribes first played the rasp with their songs. Many Plains tribes liked the idea and began using it, too. The rasp is played during dances to go along with singing and chanting.

> **Native Wisdom** *Many dances, like songs, belonged to the person who made them up and could be inherited.*
>
> **Fast Fact** *We don't know what the music of the Eastern tribes was like before the white settlers arrived because these tribes were wiped out by attacks and disease.*

Rattles

Almost every Indian dance was accompanied by the music of rattles. They were made from dried gourds filled with stones, turtle shells on sticks, or rawhide attached to a stick. Some rattles were made from buffalo horns; some from shells. After settlers arrived, Indians began making rattles from tin cans. Using whatever material was available, they created rattles to match the rhythm of a dancer or drummers.

Native Wisdom *Songs and dances had to be performed correctly. If a mistake was made, it might mean bad luck for the dancer or the tribe. Sometimes the dancer or singer who made a mistake was punished.*

Gourd Rattle:
Poke 2 holes in a dried gourd. Put in a few pebbles. Push a long stick through. Wrap and glue twine at the holes to hold the stick.

Gourd Rattle

Indians used dried gourds attached to sticks for rattles. The dried seeds made a nice sound inside. The smooth outside of the gourd was easy to paint designs on.

If you don't have a dried gourd, you can easily make a rattle from papier-mâché that looks like a gourd one.

Blow up the balloon and tape it to an end of the tube. Tear the newspaper into 1-by-4-inch strips. Mix the flour and water in the bowl to make a thin paste. Add water to thin it if necessary. Dip the newspaper strips in the paste and layer it smoothly over the balloon and tube. Cover it with at least 3 layers. Be sure to cover the end of the tube, too. When it is dry, poke or cut a small slit in the rattle. The balloon will pop and shrivel inside. Put in the dried beans or pebbles. Paste a few paper strips over the opening to seal it up. Paint the rattle with colorful geometric designs.

MATERIALS

Newspaper
Bathroom tissue tube
Small balloon
1 cup flour
1 cup water
¼ cup dried beans or
small pebbles
Masking tape
Bowl
Tempera paints

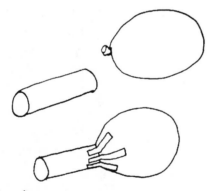

Papier-Mâché Rattle:
Tape a balloon to a paper tube.
Cover with pasted paper strips.

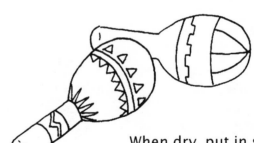

When dry, put in some
dry beans. Paint in
bright colors.

Turtle Shell Rattle

Some tribes made rattles from turtle shells. They put pebbles inside the dried shell and attached a stick for a handle. You can make a "turtle" rattle like the Onondaga people did.

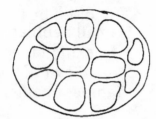

Color 2 paper plates to look like turtle shells.

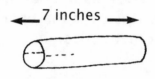

← 7 inches →

Make two 2-inch slits in a 7-inch tube.

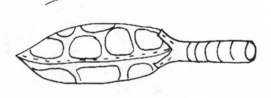

Staple the plates together, slipping in some beans. Staple the handle to the plates. Shake!

> **Native Wisdom** *Singing was thought to have magical power. This was one reason singing was so important in Native American life.*

MATERIALS

2 paper plates
½ cup dried beans
Paper towel tube
Markers, crayons, or tempera paints
Stapler
Scissors

Draw markings on the bottoms of both plates that look like a turtle's shell and color them brown and green. Staple the edges of the plates together with about an inch between each staple. When you get most of it stapled, put in the beans, and then staple it shut.

Trim the tube down to 7 inches and make two 2-inch slits across from each other at one end.

Slide the plate section between the slits and staple the handle to the plates.

Whale Rattle

The Haida people, who lived along the Northwest Coast, ate plenty of fish, but never hunted whales. They admired and respected them, hoping that they would bring them luck and strength. They carved whale rattles from wood and used them in ceremonies.

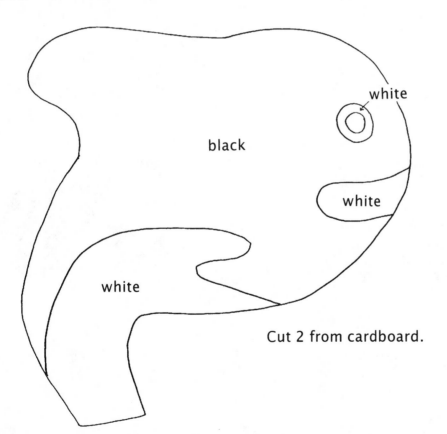

white

black

white

white

Cut 2 from cardboard.

Fast Fact *Navajo curing chants were taught from memory and were very long. If one of the singers made a mistake in the song during a curing ceremony for a sick person, the whole ceremony had to be stopped and begun again.*

Native Wisdom *North American Indians believed the animals were people like themselves—buffalo people, salmon people—and each had a tribe. The Indians worshipped the forces of nature—the sun, wind, and rain.*

Use the pattern to cut 2 whale shapes from tagboard, or draw your own. Trace and cut 1 shape, and then turn the pattern over to trace and cut the other.

Glue black paper over the tube. Flatten an end of the tube and staple it between the 2 whale shapes. Continue stapling, around the edges of the whale, keeping the staples ½ inch apart. Drop in the popcorn and staple it closed.

Use black paint to paint the whale, front and back.

MATERIALS

White tagboard
(or use an empty cereal box
and white paint)
Bathroom tissue tube
Black construction paper,
4 by 8 inches
2 tablespoons unpopped
popcorn
Pencil
Scissors
Glue
Stapler
Black tempera paint

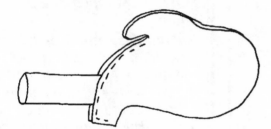

Staple the tube between the whale shapes. Add dry beans before the last few staples.

Point and shake!

Drumbeats

Good Idea *Water drums were made by some people. A log was hollowed out on one end and about an inch of water was poured inside. A hide was stretched and tied tight over the open end. The water inside changed the drum's sound and made it sound unique.*

Fast Fact *Drums were usually round, but people in the northwest part of California made and used square drums.*

Indians used drums with most dances and songs. They were made from many different things. The simplest drum was a hollow log with a piece of rawhide covering the end. The drummer tapped with his hands or a stick.

You can make your own drum out of an oatmeal box, coffee can, or plastic milk jugs.

MATERIALS

Round oatmeal box with lid,
clean coffee can with
snap-on plastic lid, or
3 plastic gallon milk jugs
If you are using milk jugs,
you will also need:
Heavy yarn
Hole punch
Sticks or dowels
Colored markers, paper,
or fabric scraps
Scissors
Glue

 Cover the box or can with colored construction paper and decorate with markers or glue on cutouts from paper or fabric scraps.

To make a drum from 3 plastic jugs, first cut away the top of 1 jug and the bottom from 2 others. Punch holes in the bottom pieces about 1 inch apart. Lace yarn through the holes to attach the 2 sections to be top and bottom of the drum. Decorate with permanent markers.

To make drumsticks, wad a scrap of cloth over an end of the stick or dowel for padding. Wrap a piece of cloth over it and tie it securely with yarn or string.

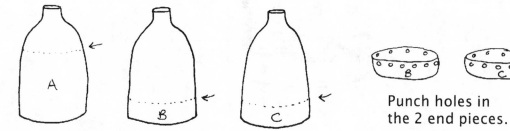

Cut 3 bottles as shown.

Punch holes in
the 2 end pieces.

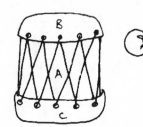

Lace the ends over the large
piece to make your drum.

Bull Roarer

This was also called a whizzer or moaning stick. The people living in the Southwest (Apache, Navajo, Pueblo, and Ute) used them to copy the sound of blowing wind. They hoped the sound would bring winds carrying rain clouds to water the dry land they lived in.

Apaches made the sticks from the wood of trees that had been struck by lightning, which they thought would have the lightning's spirit and be more likely to bring a storm.

Good Manners *Young Hopis would picnic after the sacred Kachina dances. If a girl gave a boy a plate of piki bread, which was made from blue cornmeal and ashes, it meant she was proposing marriage. Boys were careful who they went on picnics with!*

MATERIALS

Paint stirring stick (from a paint or hardware store)
Leather bootlace or
2 feet of string
Nail and hammer
Markers or paint

A paint stirring stick is long enough to cut in half and make 2 bull roarers if you want to make 1 for a friend.

Use a nail and hammer to punch a hole in the end of the stick. Remove the nail and tie an end of the bootlace to the stick.

Decorate the stick with bright colors and designs like lightning bolts, thunderbirds, clouds, and rain.

Hold on to the end of the bootlace and twirl the stick in circles above your head.

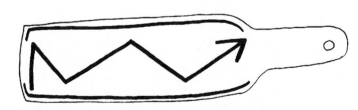

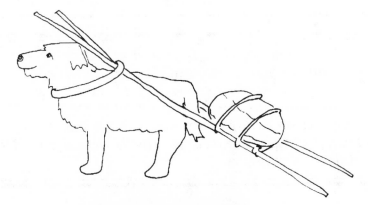

TOYS

Indian girls and boys played with toys that helped them learn how to be grown-ups. Their parents and grandparents made small baskets, pots, bows and arrows, and even tepees for the children to play with. The girls often played "house" while the boys pretended to hunt.

Little girls sometimes put puppies in toy cradleboards and carried them around pretending they were babies. A small travois was made by lashing poles together and strapping them to a dog. The children piled their toys on the travois and pretended they were moving camp with their horse.

Plains children enjoyed little villages of small tepees made by their parents. The girls worked around the pretend camp while the boys hunted. If the boys caught a prairie dog, the girls roasted it over a small fire—a little feast that delighted their parents.

Staying Alive   In most tribes, boys and girls didn't play together after they were about six years old. At that point, they spent time learning the skills they would need as grown-ups. Men and boys fished and hunted; women and girls tended gardens and made household items.

Ancient Ancestors   Native Americans didn't use the wheel until the settlers brought wagons and carts. Wheels were used in Mexico, but only on children's pull-toys.

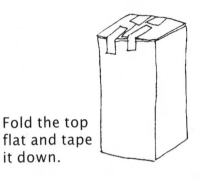

Fold the top flat and tape it down.

Cut away the center section.

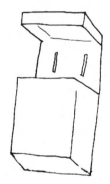

Paint or cover with paper.

MATERIALS

½-gallon milk carton
Colored paper
Old belt or
piece of woven band
Cloth large enough to wrap a
doll and fit inside the carton
Tape
Scissors
Glue

Tape the top of the carton down flat. Cut 3 sides of the carton away as shown. Cover it by gluing on pieces of colored paper. Decorate as you wish.

Cut 2 slits in the top back of the carton and slide the belt through.

Wrap a small doll in the cloth and give it a ride in the cradleboard. Wear the fastened belt across your shoulders and the cradleboard on your back.

Indian babies were tied snugly into cradleboards made of wood or baskets covered with soft animal skins and furs. Most tribes used a cradleboard baby carrier. They were handy to move baby around—like today's stroller. They gave the baby a safe place to sleep.

Little girls used toy cradleboards made by their mothers. Some were carefully decorated with hundreds of tiny beads sewn to make designs on the soft leather.

Make a cradleboard for your doll in the style used by Basin-Plateau mothers.

If you want to put a few strings of beads across the cradleboard for the doll to play with, string uncooked macaroni on some yarn. Punch holes in the carton with a sharp pencil or nail and tie the yarn ends at the sides.

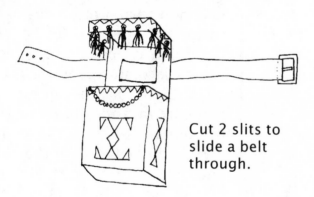

Cut 2 slits to slide a belt through.

Carry a doll in your cradleboard.

Cradle Charms

Cradleboards often had a curved hood piece to protect the baby's head. Mothers made little charms and tied them to the hood piece to spark the baby's curiosity and give her or him something to think about. They also thought the baby's future could be influenced by the charms on the cradleboard.

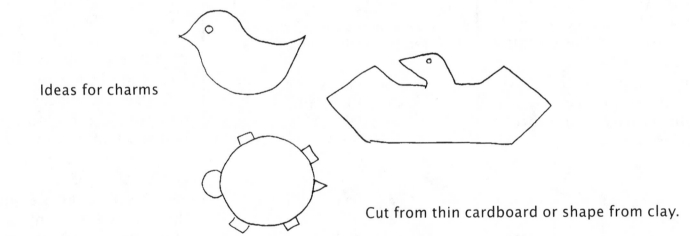

Ideas for charms

Cut from thin cardboard or shape from clay.

Corncob Doll

Indian girls played with dolls made by their mothers and grandmothers. They made them from carved sticks, hide, shells, clay—almost anything! They used human and horse hair, beads, paint, and feathers to decorate them. They carried dolls wrapped in bits of fur or hides, or on their backs in toy cradleboards. By making clothes for the dolls, the girls learned how to make clothing for their future family.

Make an easy doll from a corncob. Corn was grown in many Indian gardens before the settlers arrived.

Paint a face on the cob.

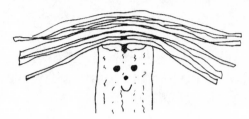

Glue yarn to the top of the cob.

Stitch and gather 2 fabric rectangles for the dress.

Cut 2 hands from chamois or felt. Glue to the edge of the cape.

Seminole Doll

Paint a face on the larger end of the cob.

Cut several pieces of yarn for hair. Use 3-inch lengths for a boy and 6 inches for a girl.

Squirt a line of glue down the center of the cob end. Lay the yarn pieces over the glue. Trim the yarn ends evenly after the glue dries. Braid the yarn if you want. Make clothing from fabric or felt scraps.

Your doll doesn't need arms, but you can cut hand shapes from felt or chamois and glue to the edge of the clothing.

To make a Seminole-style dress: Use 2 fabric rectangles, about 3 by 8 inches. (You may have to trim the dress after you are finished, depending upon the size of the corncob.) Gather both pieces along the longest edge. Use 1 for a skirt and 1 for a blouse. Sew or glue on bands of ricrac or trim along the edges. Glue hands cut from chamois to the edge of the blouse.

To make a Plains-style dress: Cut it out in 1 piece, from felt or chamois. (You can buy chamois in the auto supply section of a store. It's used to rub cars dry after washing.)

On the wrong side, sew or glue under the arms and down the sides. Turn the dress right side out. Cut a fringe at the hem. Decorate the dress with dimensional fabric paint in tubes, markers, or sew on tiny beads. Cut out hands from felt and glue inside the sleeves.

String old beads or tiny macaroni to make a necklace for your doll. A drinking straw can be cut in small pieces and strung on yarn to make a bead necklace.

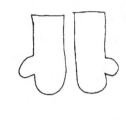

Cut hands from chamois or felt. Glue to the dress sleeves.

Plains Doll

Cut fringe at hem.

fold

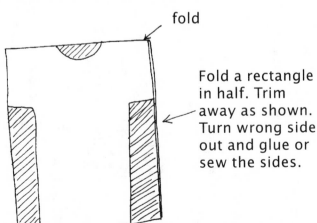

Fold a rectangle in half. Trim away as shown. Turn wrong side out and glue or sew the sides.

fold

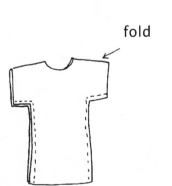

Hunting Toys

Boys were given small toy bows and arrows, tomahawks, and axes. They played while they learned how to use the hunting tools they would use to feed their family when they grew up.

Boys had to learn a lot about an animal in order to be a good hunter. They made whistles or learned to make the call of the animal. They played at being the animal, using masks. They watched and studied an animal's behavior and life cycle. All of this came in handy when they were hunting, armed with only a sharp stick or a club.

Deer Hat

Clever Indian hunters would wear the skin of an animal over their back, with the head on top of theirs. This way they could slowly and quietly sneak up on an animal. With only bows and arrows, or spears, they had to get very close to the animal. White traders brought guns with them, which made hunting much easier.

MATERIALS

2 sheets of tan construction paper, 9 by 12 inches
Brown construction paper, 3 by 20 inches
Pencil
Scissors
Stapler

❀ Draw and cut out an antler from tan paper. Turn it over and use it as a pattern for the other antler. Cut it out. Fit the strip of construction paper to your head and staple it in place. Staple the antlers in place at the sides of the headband.

Cut this pattern and then turn the pattern over to cut it the other way, so that they can go on opposite sides.

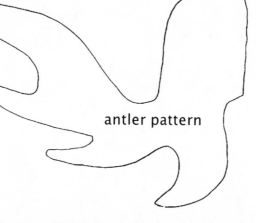

antler pattern

Staple at the sides of a paper head-band.

94

Spear

Indians made spear points by chipping away at a piece of stone with tools made of antler, bone, or stone. Obsidian was a type of stone that made very sharp spear points and knives. People traded for pieces of obsidian for chipping knife blades and arrowheads.

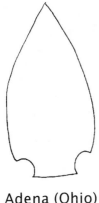

Adena (Ohio)

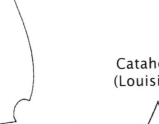

Catahoula (Louisiana)

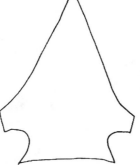

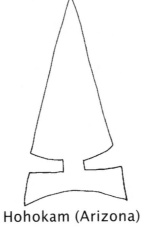

Hohokam (Arizona)

Quapaw (Arkansas)

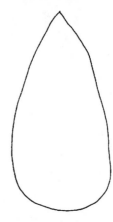

Cut from cardboard.
Can you make up a shape of your own?

MATERIALS

Cardboard from a cereal box
Paper towel tube
Construction paper
Scissors
Tape
Pencil
Glue

 Cut out a shape for your point from the cardboard. Cut 2 slits across from each other at the end of the tube. Slide the cardboard point between the slits. Wrap tape around it to hold it in place.

Draw and cut a large paper feather. Cut it into 2 pieces, right down the center. Apply glue to the cut edge of the feather and glue the feather halves across from each other at the end of the tube.

Indians in different areas made spear points in different shapes. Use one of these, or make up your own.

Make a large paper feather.

Cut it in half.

Cut 2 slits in a paper tube.

Use tape.

Glue feather halves to the tube.

Kachina Doll

MATERIALS

Cardboard from a
brown packing box
Drinking straw
Small feathers
Pencil
Heavy scissors or craft knife
(for grown-up use)
Tempera or acrylic paints,
or markers
Glue

Draw a shape on the cardboard like the one shown. Ask a grown-up to help you cut it out. Paint it the colors as shown, or make up your own.

Cut off a piece of straw about 1 inch long. Glue the straw to the face, so it stands out for a nose. Glue feathers at the top and sides of the head.

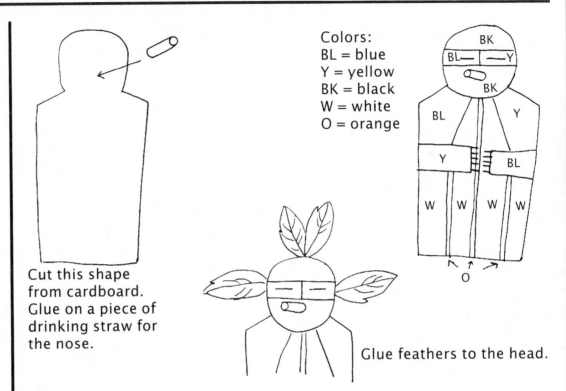

Cut this shape from cardboard. Glue on a piece of drinking straw for the nose.

Colors:
BL = blue
Y = yellow
BK = black
W = white
O = orange

Glue feathers to the head.

Kachina dolls were made for Hopi children in the Southwest by grown-ups to help teach them about the 200 to 500 different Kachina spirits that lived high in the mountains. Kachinas were believed to talk to the gods, so Hopis asked the different Kachinas to help them in various ways.

Kachina dolls were carved from the root of a cottonwood tree. They were painted with paints made from soft, ground-up clays. Men usually were the ones that made them.

At first Kachina dolls were simple flat pieces of painted wood. Through the years artists added more details. Make yours as fancy as you wish.

Dog Travois

MATERIALS

Stuffed toy dog
2 long sticks, dowels,
or yardsticks
(twice as long as the dog)
Rawhide bootlaces or
heavy string
Cardboard
Hole punch

Punch holes.

The Indians who lived on the Plains traveled a lot, following the herds of buffalo they needed for food. They didn't use carts or wagons, but used a travois to carry their belongings. A travois was made by tying 2 long poles together. A person would hold the ends on their shoulders and the other ends of the poles would drag behind on the ground. Tepees and clothing were folded and tied to the poles and parfleches full of food and tools were tied on top.

Dogs pulled travois poles fastened to a halter made of strips of rawhide. After the Spanish ships brought horses to the New World, Indians were able to use horses to pull the travois piled with their belongings. Children could ride on top of the load. Some tribes made pole cages on top of the travois for young children to ride in, so they wouldn't fall off and get hurt during travel.

You can make one to use with a stuffed toy dog. Get 2 long sticks, about twice as long as your dog. You can use dowels or yardsticks. Tie them together with a rawhide bootlace or heavy string. Tie the sticks together above the dog's head to make a sort of "x." Punch 4 holes in a piece of cardboard and tie it to the other ends of the sticks. Use rawhide or thin rope to tie the travois in position across the toy dog's chest as shown.

You can sit a little doll on the travois for your toy dog to pull.

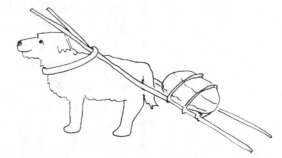

Spinning Top

The top was a favorite toy for most Indian children. Their toy tops were made from wood, horn, stone, or clay. They were decorated with brightly colored designs. Some tops were spun with whips on the frozen ice in winter.

Parents made special tops for their children, but sometimes kids made little ones themselves by pushing a stick through an acorn, or whatever was handy.

You can make a top like ones made of wood by the Gros Ventre people of Montana.

> **Fast Fact** *Native Americans caught and tamed wild horses that wandered north from the herds in Mexico brought by boat from Spain.*

Cut out a cardboard circle. Trace around a jar lid or drinking glass to get a circle.
Decorate it with colorful designs.

Punch a hole in the center with a large nail. Push a pencil through.

Twirl on a flat surface. Make lots of them in different sizes. Which spins the longest?

MATERIALS

Cardboard circle,
3 inches in diameter
Sharp pencil
Markers or paints
Nail

Decorate the cardboard with colorful design. Poke a hole with the nail in the center of the cardboard circle. Push the pencil through until about 2 inches sticks out of the cardboard. On a smooth surface, twirl the eraser end to make it spin.

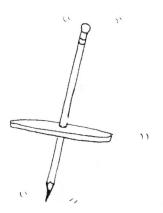

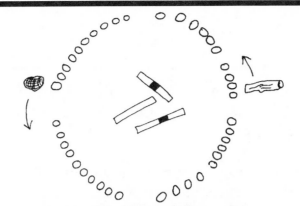

GAMES

People everywhere have always enjoyed making up and playing games. They were taught to children, who remembered them and taught them to their children. Games have been played for learning, for entertainment, or for worship.

Many different games have been passed down by Indian ancestors. Games were played in all tribes, by both grown-ups and children. A lot of time was spent making the game pieces, learning the rules, and practicing the skills to be good at the games. They liked games of chance with dice made of things they found around them. They liked games played in teams, such as ball games. They also played games of skill that kept them strong for the work they needed to do, like hunting.

Sometimes only certain people could play a game. Perhaps it was only for girls, or only for warriors. Some games could only be played at certain times of the year.

Many of the games are like those played today, in fact, some of our games had their beginnings many years ago when Native Americans began playing them.

> **Native Wisdom**   Many Indian games were based on or were part of religion. They played them as part of worship.

Hubbub

MATERIALS

5 plastic milk bottle caps
Small basket or margarine tub
50 counting sticks
(popsicle sticks)
Black, fine-point
permanent marker

 Use the marker to draw designs on the caps. Make 2 alike (x's), and make the other 3 different (stars). Leave the other side of each cap blank.

To play, put the caps in the basket and toss them in the air. Let them fall to the ground and then count up the points. Keep score like the Arapaho did:

POINTS

1 OF EITHER	0
2 X'S	3
3 STARS & 2 BLANKS	3
2 X'S & 3 BLANKS	3
4 MARKED SIDES UP	1
5 BLANK SIDES UP	1
5 MARKED SIDES UP	8

Remember that they knew all this by memory!

 Take turns tossing the dice and count up your points after each throw. Take as many counting sticks as you earned points. When all 50 counting sticks are gone, count them up to see which player has the most.

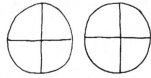

Decorate 5 caps.
Make 3 alike and
2 different.

The Arapaho of Oklahoma enjoyed this game. It was played by many other tribes and called by many different names. The dice they used were made from bones or plum pits.

Toss them in a basket.
Keep score with counting sticks.

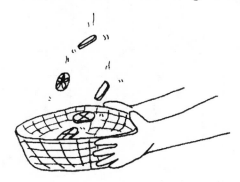

Stick Game

MATERIALS

4 popsicle sticks
12 counting sticks (toothpicks)
Red or black fine-point
permanent marker

Decorate 4 sticks with red or black pens. Only decorate one side.

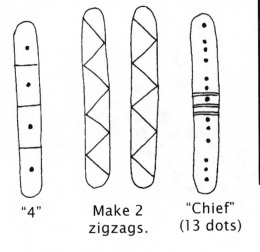

"4"   Make 2
          zigzags.   "Chief"
                        (13 dots)

 Mark 1 side of each popsicle stick with a design as shown. Leave the other side of each stick blank.

Two people can play, or 2 teams can play sitting in lines facing each other. Each player plays against the person sitting across from her or him.

Use the 12 toothpicks for keeping score. Place them in a pile on the ground between the 2 players.

To play, hold the 4 stick dice in 1 hand and drop them to the ground.

Count up your score according to the number of points for each stick combination. Take that many counting sticks.

Keep tossing the sticks and earning counting sticks until you throw a toss that counts zero points. Then it's the other player's turn.

When the counting sticks are all taken from the pile on the ground, players should begin taking them from each other's pile. The first player (or team) to earn all 12 sticks wins the game.

People of the Blackfoot nation in Montana played this stick game. They used 4 bones (actually buffalo ribs), and they kept score with 12 counting sticks.

You can make a set for playing the stick game with your friends.

Points

$$\text{OOO} + \text{🪵} = 6$$

$$\text{🪵🪵} + \text{🪵} + \text{🪵} = 4$$

$$\text{OO} + \text{🪵} + \text{🪵} = 2$$

$$\text{OO} + \text{🪵} + \text{🪵} = 0$$

$$\text{O} + \text{🪵} + \text{🪵} + \text{🪵} = 0$$

Fast Fact *When the winter ice began to melt in the spring, Cheyenne children threw their winter toys (tops, for example) into the river water. They let the water carry away all their winter toys, because winter games were not played in the summer. What would happen to our rivers if children did that today?*

Bowl Game

MATERIALS

6 plastic milk bottle caps
(all the same color)
Large flat bowl or pie pan
48 counting sticks (toothpicks
or popsicle sticks)
Permanent marker

Many tribes played a game of tossing dice in a wooden bowl and keeping score with counting sticks. You and a friend can play, just as the Passamaquoddy people in Maine did.

 Draw a different design on 1 side of each cap. Leave the other sides blank.

To play, toss the bowl full of caps in the air and catch them in the bowl. Count each cap with a design up as 1 point; blank sides amount to zero. Keep score by taking counting sticks from the pile. When the 48 counting sticks are gone, count them up and see who has the most.

The Indians had a very complicated way to count points with each combination of designs and blanks earning a different number of points.

Grown-ups spent hours at the game and often gambled, putting up their horses, houses, and all they owned to the winner of the game.

Decorate 6
different caps.

Toss them
in the bowl.

Keep score with counting sticks.
Blank sides count for zero.

Throw Sticks

This game was played by Apaches in the Southwest. To make a set for 2 players:

 Color each of the sticks solid yellow with a green stripe across the middle.

Arrange the 40 stones in a large circle (about 5 feet in diameter). Lay them in 4 groups of 10 as shown.

Place the 2 place markers across from each other.

To play, toss the 3 sticks down in the center of the circle. Count up the points according to the way the sticks land. Move your place marker around the circle, passing 1 stone for each point.

The other player does the same, moving his or her marker in the same direction. If a person's marker lands on or passes another's marker the person passed over must go all the way back to the starting spot.

The first player to move around the circle past all 40 stones wins the game.

MATERIALS

3 tongue depressors or paint stirring sticks
40 small stones or dry lima beans
Green and yellow crayons or markers
2 place markers
(Use small sticks, feathers, shells, or whatever you want.)

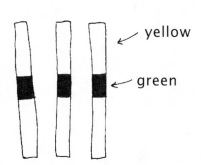

← yellow

← green

POINTS	
3 BLANK SIDES UP	10
2 BLANK SIDES UP, 1 STRIPED UP	1
1 BLANK SIDE UP, 2 STRIPED UP	3
3 STRIPED UP	5

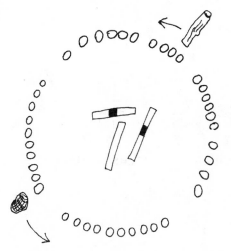

Wooden Dice

This game was played by Apache warriors. You can play with your own set, and 2 or 4 players.

Paint all the dice black on 1 side. When they are dry, paint 3 of them brown on the other side and 10 of them white.

To play, fold the towel to make a cushion to strike the basket against. (Apaches dug a small hole in the ground, lined it with leafy branches and placed a blanket over it, to cushion the basket while playing.)

Lay all 13 dice in the basket. Hold onto both sides and bring it down sharply, hitting the bottom of the basket against the towel. The force will toss the dice, turning them over to land in the basket.

Count scores for the number of sides up:

The complicated scoring patterns had to be remembered by all the players—it wasn't written down!

MATERIALS

13 small pieces of wood
(1 by 1½ inches) or
small bottle caps
Bath towel or pillow
Flat basket or pie pan
Black, brown, and white paint

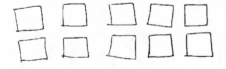

Paint 10 pieces white.

Paint 3 pieces brown.

WHITE	BLACK	BROWN	POINTS EARNED
3	10	0	12
0	10	3	10
0	12	1	10
5	8	0	10
7	6	0	10
10	0	3	20
10	3	0	16
3	7	3	5
10	1	2	5

Fast Fact *Early traders had difficulty buying game pieces from Indians. They wouldn't sell the stick, bone, or bead dice because they felt that they would be selling the right to play the game again, unless the buyer gave them permission.*

Strike the basket against the towel to toss the dice.

Shell Dice

MATERIALS

4 flat shells,
2 a bit larger than the others
(You can also use coins,
bottle caps, or circles
cut from heavy cardboard.)
Blanket
10 counting sticks (toothpicks)

✿Prepare the dice if you aren't using real shells. Paint or make a mark on 1 side of each die. If you use coins, let the imprints be your markings. If using real shells, points are determined by whether the shell lands with the rounded (convex) or sunken (concave) side up.

To play, toss the 4 dice onto the blanket with your hand. Count the score and take that many counting sticks. Then the other player tosses and counts up a score. When the 10 counting sticks are gone, players take them from each other. The game ends when 1 player holds all 10 sticks.

SHELL CURVES OVER (HEADS)	SHELL CURVES UNDER (TAILS)	POINTS
2	2	4
4	0	1
0	4	1

No other combinations count for points.

Use shells for dice, or use bottle caps.

2 over + 2 under = 4 points

The Hupa people of northern California played this game. They used mussel shells or pieces of abalone shell.

This is a game for 2 players.

> **Native Wisdom** Indians kept track of time by watching the world around them. Days were counted by sleeps (or nights). Months were counted by moons. Years were counted by winters. A person's age was counted by the winters in her or his lifetime.

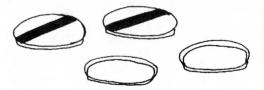

2 marked + 2 unmarked = 4 points

Stick Dice

MATERIALS

6 tongue depressors
or popsicle sticks
Woodburning tool
(with grown-up help) or
a brown permanent marker
12 counting sticks (toothpicks)
Pencil

The Pomo Indians of California played this game.

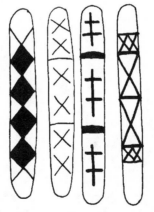Draw a design on 1 side of each flat stick. The Indians burned their designs into the wood. You can use a woodburning tool to trace over your pencil lines or use a marking pen to color the design.

To play, 2 players take turns tossing the stick dice onto the ground and counting the score. Keep score by taking counting sticks from a pile on the ground.

No other combinations count. The first player to earn all 12 counting sticks is the winner. Women played this game for hours. Small sets were made to give to children for toys.

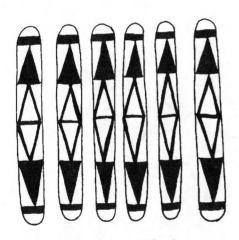

Decorate 6 sticks with the same design.

Here are some other design ideas people used.

BLANK SIDE UP	DECORATED SIDE UP	POINTS
6	0	2
0	6	3
3	3	1

Walnut Shell Game

MATERIALS

6 walnut half shells
½ cup salt-dough or clay
Colored paper scraps
Pencil
Scissors
Glue

 Press the clay into each shell, making it firm and flattening it smooth. Use a pencil to trace around the flat side of the shell on the colored paper. Cut out and glue it to the flat side of the shell.

Four players take turns tossing the dice. A fifth keeps score with the 15 tally sticks.

Toss the shells in the basket and score:

POINTS

All flat side up, or all flat
  side down = 1

3 flat sides up & 3 flat
  sides down = 2

No other combinations
  score points.

> **Fast Fact**   *The Uinkaret Indians of Arizona made playing cards out of flat pieces of tree bark. They marked them with different painted designs.*

This was played by the Yokut Indians of central California. They gathered wild acorns and walnuts for food, and used the shells to make game pieces. The Yokuts filled the empty half shells with pine pitch and pressed pretty pieces of abalone shell into the pitch. The women wove a flat basket tray for a playing table.

Fill walnut half shells with clay and toss in a basket.

Kainsish

The Maricopa people of Arizona used 4 pieces of cane that represented the earth, moon, sky, and sun.

MATERIALS

4 tongue depressors or popsicle sticks
Red marker, crayon, or paint

Color all the sticks red on 1 side. On the other side, draw designs that represent the earth, moon, sky, and sun—one on each stick.

To play, take turns tossing the sticks to the ground and counting the score:

POINTS

4 red sides up = 1
4 marked sides up = 2
All other throws are zero.

Count the score by marking it in the dust like the Indians did, or use a pencil and paper. The first player to earn 6 points wins.

Decorate 4 sticks with designs for the earth, moon, sky, and sun. Color the back of each stick red.

Earth   Moon   Sky   Sun

Stick Counting Game

Piegan children in Montana played this game. Use straws, sticks, toothpicks, or pencils. You need at least 13, but can use as many as you like as long as the total is an uneven number.

One player divides the sticks into 2 bundles with 1 bundle having 1 more stick than the other. The other player then tries to pick the bundle that has 1 more.

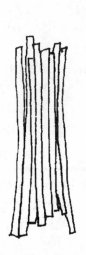 

Quick! Which bundle has more?
Guess first, and then count carefully.
Were you correct?

Hidden Stick Game

Chun Wiyushnanpi was the name of this game the Teton Dakota children played. They used sumac sticks; you can use toothpicks, coffee stirrers, or popsicle sticks. Use a marker to put a little dot on 1 stick. To play, 1 person mixes up the sticks, closes her or his eyes, and then divides the sticks into 2 piles. The first player puts her or his hands over both piles so that the marked stick cannot be seen. The other player selects 1 of the piles. Both players look over their sticks and the one who has the marked stick wins.

Hand Game

Eighty-one different tribes played this game! It could be played by people who didn't speak each other's language by using only sign language.

The game was played inside a wigwam or tepee. Men and boys, and women and girls, played the game in separate groups.

> **Fast Fact** *While playing hand games, Indians would chant lively songs that grew louder and faster until the player made his or her guess.*

MATERIALS

Button, bead, shell, stone, or small piece of bone
6 counting sticks (toothpicks)

The 2 players sit on the ground facing each other. The first player switches the button or other small object back and forth between his or her hands several times to confuse the other player. The first player makes 2 fists and the other player guesses which hand holds the hidden button.

If the second player guesses correctly, he or she takes a counting stick, and then takes a turn hiding the button while the first player guesses.

Players continue, taking counting sticks from each other until 1 player holds all 6 sticks.

Traditional game pieces for the Hand Game.

bone and cord

beads
bone

bone

Not-so-traditional game pieces

coin
button
pasta
bean

Moccasins

The Santee Dakota people of Minnesota played this guessing game.

Make 3 paper moccasins like the ones Woodland people made from skins.

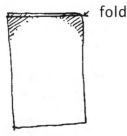

Fold a piece of 8½-by-11-inch paper in half. Trim off the corners.

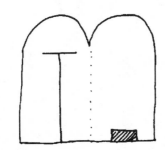

Open and cut a "T" in one half and a rectangle in the other.

Decorate the "T" side with crayons or markers. Woodland people used flower designs.

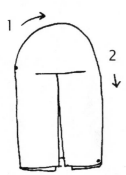

Glue together along the edge between 1 and 2.

Fold the corners of the rectangle to the center and tape.

MATERIALS

3 moccasins or shoes
Small ball or stick

A player hides the ball inside 1 of the 3 moccasins. The other player guesses which one it's in. He gets 2 guesses. If he loses, he trades places and hides the ball.

Fast Fact *During the wet winter weather, Coeur d'Alene Indian children's moccasins were made from the skins of large salmon, which kept their feet dry.*

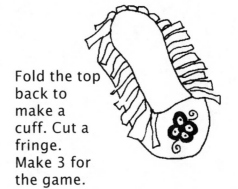

Fold the top back to make a cuff. Cut a fringe. Make 3 for the game.

Feathered Darts

 Cut a large triangle shape from the side of the box. Roll it into a cone and staple or tape it to hold securely.

Cut out 2 paper feathers and staple or tape them to the wide end of the cone.

Toss the darts with the narrow end in front.

MATERIALS

Cereal box
Colored paper
Scissors
Stapler
Tape

The Mandan and Hidatsa children of North Dakota made darts from deer antlers and feathers. They slid them along the ground to see who could make theirs go farthest. This was played on frozen snow or ice in the winter.

Roll and tape the cardboard into a cone.

Make paper feathers and staple them to the cone.

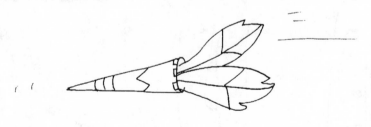

Toss it to see who can throw the farthest!

Hoop and Lances

The Miska of British Columbia propped a hoop up and threw sticks or lances aimed inside the hoop. This helped young hunters practice their aiming and throwing skills.

MATERIALS

Willow branch or
wire coat hanger
Heavy tape
Heavy cardboard
(from cardboard boxes)

Make a hoop by taping a length of willow branch or a wire coat hanger into a circle. Prop the hoop in a doorway. Cut lances from the cardboard. Stand back and try to toss them into the hoop.

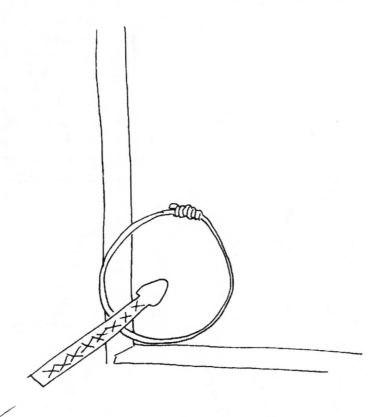

Hoop and Darts

MATERIALS

Flexible tree branch,
coat hanger, or small hoop
Heavy tape
Yarn or heavy cord
Wooden clothespins
Feathers (real or paper)
Glue or rubber bands

You can use a small hoop made from a tree branch, an embroidery hoop, or a coat hanger. Hold the ends in place with masking tape. Wrap yarn or heavy cord across the hoop as shown. Prop it against a tree or wall, or hang by a cord from a tree branch.

Make darts by fastening feathers to the ends of wooden clothespins with glue or rubber bands.

To play, toss the darts through the hoop. Points are scored for the ones that go through.

The Paiute people (from Utah) played hoop and darts. They used a small hoop that was about 7 inches across.

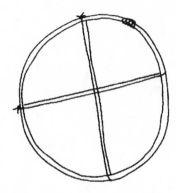

Tie yarn to the hoop.

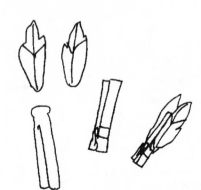

Glue feathers
to clothespins.

Good Idea *Native Americans were the first to swim using the crawl stroke. In the nineteenth century, two American Indians won Olympic medals in a freestyle event. They swam using the crawl and made their competitors mad because they thought it was unfair, since no one had done it before. When swimmers saw how successful the crawl was, others began using it.*

Buzz

For centuries, Indian children all over the West and Alaska played with whirling toys made from flat pieces of bone, pottery, or gourd shell. They drilled holes in the center of the flat piece and threaded it with a strip of cord or sinew. When they held the cord in each hand and twisted it, the piece of bone whirled through the air and made a buzzing sound.

MATERIALS

Large flat button with 2 holes
Heavy thread, 36 inches long

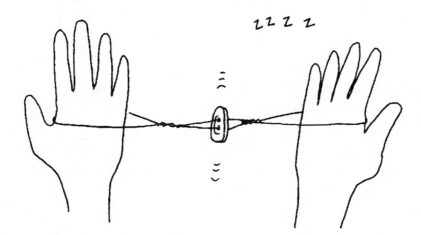
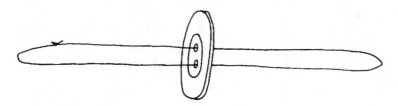

Run the thread through both holes and knot the ends, creating a large loop.

To play, put your fingers through the loop, stretch it out with the button in the center, and twirl the button so that the string twists at 1 end. Keep twirling until several inches of thread is twisted. Make the button spin by moving your hands in and out, letting the thread unwind quickly. You can hear a buzzing sound as it whirls around on the thread.

Pin and Target

MATERIALS

¼-inch stick, dowel, or pencil
Yarn or string, 24 inches long
Cardboard circle,
3 inches in diameter, or
plastic lid (Ask a grown-up to
cut holes in it with a craft knife.)
Markers or crayons
Scissors
Hole punch

Tie 1 end of the yarn to the end of the stick with a tight knot.

Make targets by punching several holes in the cardboard target. Make the largest hole in the center, using the hole punch several times to make it bigger than the other holes.

Decorate it with markers if you want.

Tie the end of the yarn to the target.

To play, hold the stick, toss the target into the air, and catch it on the stick. Make up your own point system.

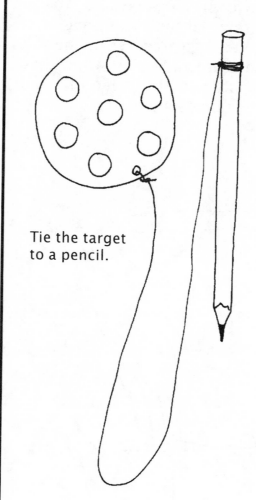

Tie the target to a pencil.

Many tribes made these for children and adults. The Algonquian used bones for targets. The Pima used pumpkin rinds, and the Penobscot used balls made of moose hair. They used whatever was available to make the target.

You can make yours from whatever you have around the house, too.

Toss and catch the target with the pencil.

Racket Ball

MATERIALS

4 plastic 2-liter bottles
(2 for each player)
Newspaper
Masking tape
Scissors

Cut the bottles as shown to make scoops for tossing and catching. Make a simple ball by firmly wadding newspaper into a 4-inch ball shape and wrapping tape around it.

To play, use 1 scoop for tossing and catching and the other for helping keep the ball from falling.

If you have several players, divide yourselves into 2 teams. Mark out 2 lines at the ends of a playing field. Each team tries to throw the ball to each other as they run toward their goal line, getting the ball across the line before the other team takes it.

Different Indian villages used to travel to play racket ball with each other, and often bet their belongings on the game's outcome.

People used to play this game each spring where the city of La Crosse, Wisconsin, is now located. We now play a similar game called "lacrosse."

The Miwok of California called this game "Amtah." They used woven baskets with handles to catch and toss a ball made out of hide stuffed with hair.

Make a set to play with someone else.

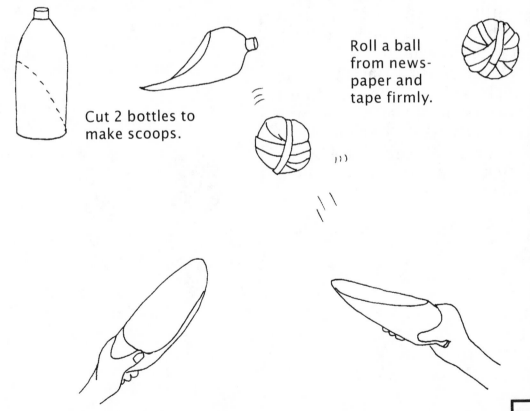

Cut 2 bottles to make scoops.

Roll a ball from newspaper and tape firmly.

Shinny

Almost all the tribes played this game. They used a curved stick to hit a ball along the ground like in hockey. The ball was made from wood, stone, or hide.

Teams tried to take the ball across the goal line at the ends of a playing field. Players could kick the ball or hit it with sticks, but couldn't touch it with their hands.

You can use a small ball and stick to play. If you can't find a stick, you can make a strong one by cutting out pieces of heavy cardboard in a hockey stick shape and taping them together.

Tape cardboard pieces together to make a shinny stick.

Fast Fact *A Choctaw game of ball could have 600 to 1,000 players. Crowds of up to 5,000 people watched along the sidelines. The ball field was about half a mile long. People camped beside the ball field during the games.*

Fast Fact *In the past, there was pushing, pulling, biting, and broken bones during a shinny game. Spectators would bet their belongings on the winning team. Slow players could be whipped by spectators who wanted their team to win.*

Ball Race

The ball race was played by Southwestern tribes. They used balls of stone, wood, or cow's horn. Sometimes they used sticks instead of balls.

MATERIALS

2 empty cans
Red cloth tape or
red acrylic paint

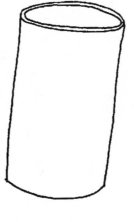

Mark one can with a stripe of red tape or paint.

Mark 1 can with a stripe of red tape, or paint around the middle.

Play with 2 teams, each using 1 of the cans. Draw 2 goal lines at the ends of the playing field, or spread out 2 blankets, like the Indian teams did.

Kick the cans with your feet. No hands allowed! The first team to get theirs across the goal line or onto their blanket wins. Teams can be large, because some players will be kicking their own team's can while others try to kick the other team's can away from their goal.

Juggling

The Eskimo, Bannock, Shoshone, and Ute people enjoyed juggling. They learned as children and could juggle three to five items at once. They used stones or balls shaped from clay.

Find 3 smooth stones and paint them as you wish. Juggle by tossing 1 stone up in the air as you pass another from 1 hand to the other, and toss a third stone up into the air. Start with 2 stones; when you can handle them, add another. Can you juggle 5?

Shoshone jugglers used to race while juggling. The first player to run to a chosen tree while juggling—without dropping a stone—won.

Good Idea *Pimas and Maricopas of Arizona used the inner pulp from a sunflower stalk as chewing gum.*

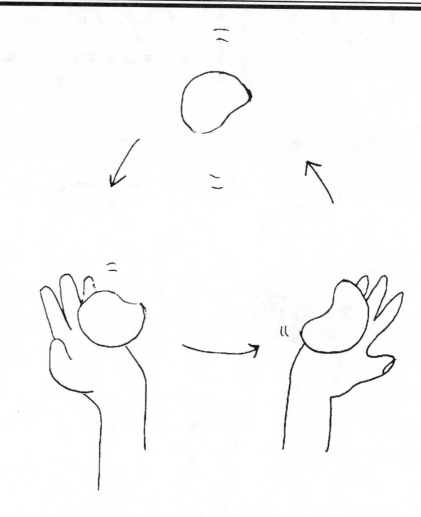

126

Pokean

The Zunis of Arizona invented this game.

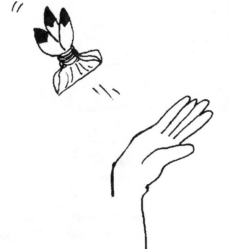

MATERIALS

Dried corn husks or strips cut
from a paper bag
Feathers
(real or cut from paper)
Rubber bands

✿ Lay the corn husks on top of each other crosswise, bringing the ends up and fastening them with a rubber band.

Attach 3 feathers securely between the rubber bands.

To play, bat it into the air with your hand. Keep batting it back up into the air, counting the number of times you can hit it before you miss and it falls to the ground. 10 is the usual goal, but some players could make 50 or 100 hits before dropping the game piece.

Standing Cob Game

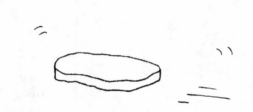Use an empty tissue tube and 2 paper plates stapled together at the edges. Decorate them with colorful designs if you want. Stand back and toss the plates, trying to knock the tube over.

MATERIALS

Empty tissue tube
2 paper plates
Stapler
Markers or crayons

The Zuni of New Mexico played this game with thin disks of sandstone and a corn cob. If you don't have flat stones and a corn cob, you can make your own pieces.

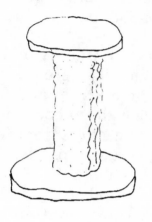

Indians used a cob and sandstone disks.

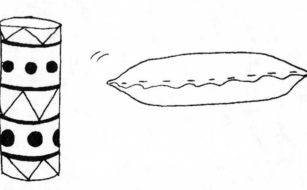

You can use paper plates and a tissue tube. Toss the disk to knock over the tube.

Cat's Cradle

Many tribes played games by twisting cord loops around their hands into clever shapes and designs.

The Zuni said that these designs were the netted shields of the War Gods. They said the War Gods learned to make these from their grandmother, the Spider.

The Navajos said the Spider people invented the game. The game could only be played in winter when spiders are hibernating and can't see people playing it. If a person played it any other time of the year, they would have very bad luck!

The children twisted cord to create designs representing twin stars, lightning, turtles, deer, beavers, humming birds, butterflies, and bats. What can you invent?

Loop string around your thumbs and little fingers.

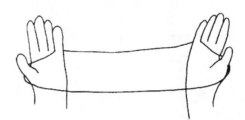

Put your first finger through the loop across each palm.

Spread your hands apart, and you have a "cat's cradle." Can you make up your own designs?

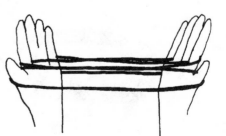

Ring Toss

This game was played by Zuni boys in New Mexico. They made the rings by wrapping twigs with yarn. You and a friend can play, or you can practice your aiming skills alone.

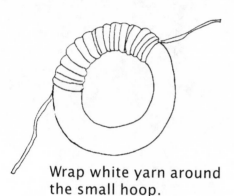

Wrap white yarn around the small hoop.

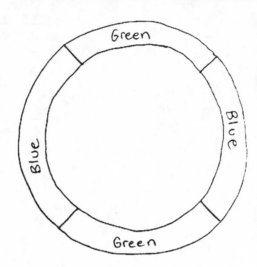

Wrap the large hoop with blue and green yarn.

MATERIALS

2 plastic lids,
1 larger than the other
White, green, and blue
yarn scraps
Scissors

 Save 2 plastic lids from food containers like yogurt, coffee, shortening, cottage cheese, or whipped topping. One should be larger than the other. Use scissors (or ask a grown-up to use a craft knife) to cut out the center, leaving a plastic ring.

Wrap and knot white yarn around the smaller ring. Wrap and knot green and blue yarn in 4 sections around the larger ring.

To play, toss the larger hoop down on the ground. Then aim carefully and try to toss the smaller hoop so it lands inside the larger.

If the ring lands inside, the player gets 2 points. If it lands on a green section, it counts 1 point. Landing on blue gets zero.

Try to toss the small hoop inside the large one.

Foot Races

Indians enjoyed running—it kept them fast for hunting, and they liked to compete with other villages.

A Pima village (Arizona) would challenge another village to a race by sending a messenger to tell them that in five days they would like to meet for a race. They began singing and dancing to prepare. Boys trained by running in groups of five. Each village had about 40 or 50 runners.

On the day of the race, half of the runners went to each end of the track. They ran in relays, handing willow sticks to waiting runners. The 2 sides raced back and forth until a team was so far ahead the other couldn't catch up or until a team admitted they were too tired to run anymore.

A Mandan race track was 3 miles long, which they ran over 3 times!

Staying Alive *Being a fast runner was important in Native American villages. It was honored next to being a warrior or hunter.*

Fast Fact *In order to run faster, Mandan racers wore only moccasins and paint. Winners got red feathers they turned in for prizes people had wagered. Races were held in summer and fall, before the hunting season.*

"WHAT'S FOR DINNER?"

When the Europeans came to the New World, they found people were eating unusual foods that they had never seen or tasted before. They had never seen corn, potatoes, tomatoes, or melons—all grown in Indian gardens. Indians also showed them how to grow beans, squash, and pumpkins.

> ***Good Idea*** *Tomatoes were considered weeds until early farmers began tending them as garden crops.*
>
> ***Depending on Plants*** *When Columbus landed in the New World, he discovered people tending cornfields 18 miles long. He had never even eaten corn before.*

Fry Bread

Mix the dry ingredients together in a bowl. Add the oil and water. Dust your hands with flour to keep them from getting sticky. Knead the dough until it's stretchy, but not sticky. Pull off a clump the size of a plum and roll it into a ball with your hands.

Pat the dough ball between your hands until it's flat. Then begin gently pulling the dough to stretch it out until it's shaped like a thin, flat pancake. This takes a bit of practice. If you can't get yours stretched, lay it on a surface dusted with flour and roll it flat with a rolling pin.

Punch a hole through the center with your thumb. This hole will help the bread cook evenly.

Ask an adult to fry the bread in a few inches of hot cooking oil. When 1 side turns a light brown color, turn it over with 2 forks and cook the other side.

Flatten it and punch a hole in the center with your thumb.

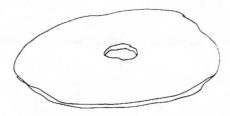

INGREDIENTS

2 cups flour
2 teaspoons baking powder
½ teaspoon salt
1 tablespoon oil
¾ cup water
Cooking oil

UTENSILS

Bowl
Rolling pin (optional)
Frying pan
Paper towels

This is a very popular Indian food today. It is made and sold throughout the country. You can cover fry bread with powdered sugar, honey, hot chili, or salsa. It's a traditional food of the Navajo people, but many other tribes enjoy it, too. So will you!

This recipe makes 8 to 10 pieces.

Be careful around hot oil. An adult must help.

Put the hot bread on a plate covered with a paper towel to drain and cool.

Sprinkle the bread with powdered sugar and drizzle it with honey for a sweet treat. To make a meal, spoon hot chili, beans, or stew onto the bread, and eat.

Fast Fact *In most tribes, stew was always cooking over the fire and people ate whenever they were hungry.*

They used a large buffalo horn or wooden ladle to fill bowls made of clay, wood, shell, or tightly woven baskets. People used spoons made from wood or horn, or they tipped the bowls to their mouths.

Let a grown-up deep fry the bread until it's golden brown.
Top with honey and powdered sugar.
Yummy!

Honey

Kneel-Down Bread

This bread got its name from the way Pueblo women kneeled to grind corn with stone tools. The stone held in the hand is called a "mano," and the flat stone the corn was ground on is called a "metate."

This doesn't really taste or look like bread. It's more like a pudding wrapped in corn husks. Use fresh corn on the cob. Two ears will make several portions. Husk the corn and save the larger pieces of husk.

 Use a table knife or serrated plastic knife to scrape the kernels off the ear. Put the corn kernels into a large bowl and begin mashing them with your hands. (Indian women would have ground the corn with a stone.) You can grind the kernels very quickly with a blender if you want.

Pour off the liquid from the kernels. Spoon about 1 or 2 tablespoons of mashed corn pulp onto a piece of husk. Roll the husk up around the corn and place the little "package" on a cookie sheet. You can make several packages.

Bake at 350°F for 1 hour. After it cools a little, unroll the husk, spoon out the cooked corn, and eat.

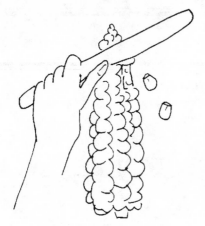

Cut corn off the cob.

Spoon the corn mixture onto a piece of husk.

Roll it up and bake. Unwrap and eat! (Don't eat the husk. It's a natural disposable wrapper!)

Baked Pumpkin

 Wash and dry the pumpkin. Put it on a cookie sheet and bake at 350°F for about 2 hours.

Take the pumpkin out of the oven, and don't turn off the oven. When the pumpkin is cool enough to touch, cut the top off (like a Jack-o-Lantern) and scoop out the seeds and pumpkin pulp. Put the pulp in a large bowl. Save the seeds for roasted pumpkin seeds, page 152.

Mix the cider, syrup, and margarine in a small bowl, pour it into the large bowl with the pulp, and mix it with the spoon.

Pour all of this into the pumpkin shell, and put it back in the oven to bake for 35 minutes. When it's cool, cut it into pieces to eat.

This was eaten by Ojibwa families, who grew pumpkins and tapped maple trees for syrup—a delicious combination!

INGREDIENTS

Small pumpkin
¼ cup apple cider
¼ cup maple syrup
¼ cup melted margarine

UTENSILS

Cookie sheet
Large spoon
Large bowl
Knife

Good Idea *The Cocopas of the Southwest ground up pumpkin seed kernels to use as a hand cream or mix with face paint.*

Bake the pumpkin.
Then cut the top off.

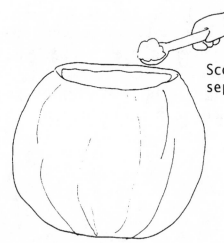

Scoop out the pulp and
separate the seeds.

Mix cider, syrup, margarine,
and pumpkin pulp in a bowl.
Put it all back in the pumpkin
and bake. The pumpkin shell
is the baking dish!

Corn and Pumpkin Stew

 Use the knife to cut the corn kernels off the cob. (Save the cob to make a corn cob doll, page 92.)

Cut the pumpkin open and scoop the seeds out of the pumpkin. Save them for roasted pumpkins seeds, page 152. Ask an adult to help peel and cut the pumpkin into small pieces.

Put the pumpkin pieces into the pot. Add 2 cups of water and a spoonful of salt. Simmer for about 20 minutes, until the pumpkin gets soft. Add the corn and heat. Eat it while it's still hot.

Years ago, this stew was cooked in tightly woven baskets. Large rocks were heated on the fire and dropped into the basket of food to cook it.

INGREDIENTS

3 ears corn (fresh or frozen) or 2 cans whole kernel corn, drained
Small pumpkin
2 cups water
Teaspoon salt

UTENSILS

Table knife or serrated plastic knife
Spoon
Large pot

This was eaten by the Havasupai people who lived at the bottom of the Grand Canyon in Arizona.

Native Wisdom *Some Native Americans thought the turkey was a cowardly animal. They wouldn't eat it because they were afraid they'd become cowardly like the turkey.*

Wild Rice

Wild rice was the basic food for the Chippewa people living in the Great Lakes area.

Wild rice grows in shallow lakes. It's not really rice, but the seed of a grass that grows in water.

In late summer when the rice was ripe, families would camp by the lake. They went out in canoes to gather rice. To harvest the rice, the plant stems were bent over the canoe and the rice kernels were knocked off with sticks. The rice landed in the bottom of the canoe. When the canoe was full, they headed back to camp.

Not all the rice was harvested. Some was always left to fall into the water to seed the next year's plants.

Back at camp, the rice was spread on sheets of birch bark or blankets laid on the ground, and dried for a day.

When it was dry, the rice was put in barrels made of wooden boards. It was pounded with a large pointed stick. This loosened the coarse husks from the kernels.

Next, the husks and kernels had to be separated. The rice was placed on a bark tray and tossed into the air. The heavier rice kernels would drop onto the bark spread below, and the lighter husks would blow away.

While they were at rice camp, the children helped catch fish and pick berries; hunters brought in ducks or deer.

Everything was eaten with the fresh cooked rice in a beautiful setting of tall pines, fluttering birch forests, and glistening lakes.

To cook wild rice today, you can buy a package in the gourmet section of a grocery store. It's expensive when you compare it to white rice, but it's a delicious, special treat—and it's easier than building a canoe and picking your own!

INGREDIENTS

1 cup wild rice
1 teaspoon salt
1 tablespoon margarine
2½ cups water

First rinse the rice and drain it in a colander. Put all the ingredients in a large pot. Heat to boiling. Stir a few times. Put on a lid, turn the heat down, and simmer for 45 minutes.

Good Manners   *Who washed the dishes?*
Everyone—kids and adults—was in charge of washing her or his own bowls and spoons.

Corn Soup

The Oneida people made this easy soup. Fresh corn was cut from the cob and a little deer meat was cut up and mixed in. Wild green plants like milkweed or ferns were added. A handful of wild rice was tossed in, too.

You can make today's version easily.

> **Native Wisdom** *People in the Southeast tribes used hoes made out of a bone or shell tied to a stick to work their fields of corn, beans, and squash. Lazy workers had to pay a fine.*

INGREDIENTS

1 handful fresh spinach greens, washed and drained
1 can whole kernel corn
½ cup cooked beef, cut in small pieces
1 handful rice (white, brown, or wild rice mix)
1 quart water
1 teaspoon salt

Tear the washed greens into pieces. Put everything into a large pot and simmer until the rice is cooked. (15 minutes for white rice; 30 minutes for brown rice; 45 minutes for wild rice.)

chipped stone hoe
(Northeast)

Hoes made from shells tied to sticks
(East Coast)

a hoe made from a buffalo shoulder blade tied to a stick
(Plains)

Hominy

Hominy was made by boiling corn cut from the cob in water with ashes and lime until the hulls—the protective covering—fell off the kernels.

Mohawk children ate hominy with beans and chunks of bear meat. Try this easier method.

> ***Good Manners*** *In many Indian villages, they usually ate two meals a day, the big one in the evening. If people got hungry between meals they just helped themselves. Neighbors could eat at each other's homes, if they needed to.*

INGREDIENTS

1 can hominy
1 can pinto beans
½ cup cooked ham, cut in cubes (or hot dogs, sliced)

Drain the liquid from the can of hominy. Put the hominy, beans, and ham in a pot, heat them up, and serve in bowls.

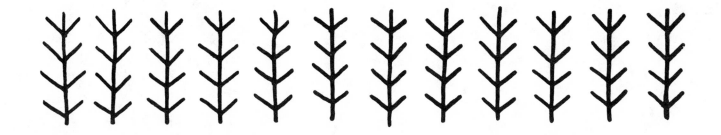

Steamed Clover

Shoshone Indians had a very hard time getting food in their harsh land. They would steam clover by laying wet clover between stacks of hot stones. It was tasty and nutritious.

You can try gathering some in your yard.

If you don't have clover, you can buy fresh spinach and cook it instead. Beet tops, collards, mustard greens, or turnip greens are fine, too.

Wash the leaves and put a handful in a small pot. Add ¼ cup water. Cover with a lid and simmer about 5 minutes.

WARNING: Ask your parents to be sure your yard hasn't been sprayed with chemicals!

> ***Staying Alive*** *The Diggers were a Shoshone group that lived in a very dry, harsh land where food was hard to find. Few animals even lived there. Sometimes the people would scare grasshoppers into a pit and beat them to death with branches. Then, they would gather them, mash them up, form cakes, and let them dry in the sun.*

Baked Squash

Many tribes raised squash in gardens. They baked butternut or acorn squash by laying it on hot coals, covering it with more hot coals, and leaving it to cook. When it was soft enough to poke a stick into it, it was done cooking. They cut it in half, scooped out the seeds, and drizzled maple syrup on it.

You can bake an acorn squash in the oven.

 Wash and dry the squash. Put it on a cookie sheet and bake it at 350°F for 35 minutes. Take it out, cut it in half, and scoop out the seeds. Throw out the seeds.

Scoop out the pulp from the skin. Put it in a bowl and add the margarine, salt, and syrup. Stir and mash with a large spoon. Add the nuts. Put the mixture into a greased casserole dish and bake at 450°F for about 20 minutes.

INGREDIENTS

Acorn squash
1 tablespoon margarine
½ teaspoon salt
2 tablespoons maple syrup (optional)
½ cup walnut or hickory nuts, chopped

UTENSILS

Cookie sheet
Knife
Spoon
Large bowl
Casserole dish

Good Manners *The Chiri-cahua Apache people had very strict eating manners. Kids didn't eat or drink until grown-ups had started. They couldn't move or wiggle during meals, or overeat.*

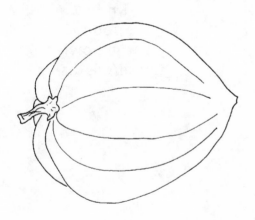

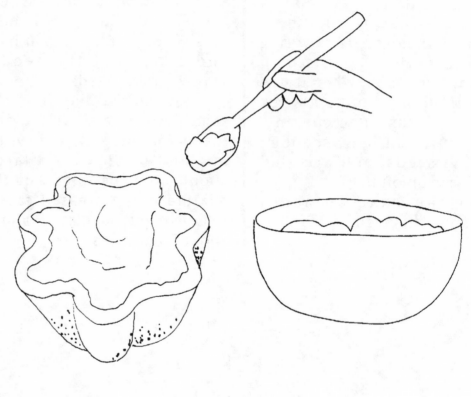

Bake the squash.
Cut it in half and
scoop out the pulp.

Fried Squash Blossoms

Indians in the Southwest grew many different kinds of squash in their gardens. To save the squash for eating in the winter they sliced it into strips, removed the seeds, and dried it in the sun.

Squash blossoms were sometimes eaten as a treat. If you have a garden or a friend with a garden, perhaps you'd like to try it. You'll never be able to order this in a restaurant!

Good Manners *When visitors were invited for a meal, they brought their own dish and spoon.*

INGREDIENTS

4 cups of fresh
squash blossoms
½ cup flour
1 cup milk
½ teaspoon salt
½ teaspoon chili powder
(optional)
Cooking oil

Pick the squash blossoms in the morning before they open completely. Mix the other ingredients into a batter and dip the blossoms in it until they're covered. Ask an adult to help you fry the battered blossoms in a frying pan with oil. Fry them until they are crisp.

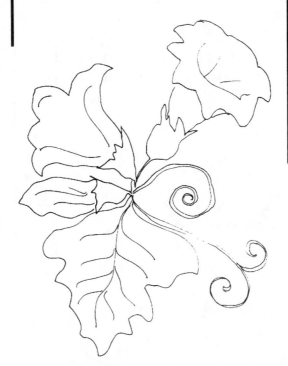

Fish Soup

Many Indians lived near oceans, lakes, rivers, and streams so they could eat fish year-round.

They caught fish with hand-knotted nets, traps woven from sticks, and small, hand-carved bone or wooden hooks. Large fish could be taken with spears or bows and arrows.

Cooks prepared fresh fish by roasting it over hot coals. Fish that they wanted to save for later was kept from spoiling by placing it on sticks over a fire where the smoke dried it. Fish was also laid in the sun to dry.

Smoked and dried fish was kept in baskets, bark boxes, or hide cases called "parfleches" (see page 24). It was added to soups and stews or eaten plain all winter long.

Here's a simple fish soup recipe that probably tastes quite a bit like that served in Indian camps long ago. You don't need to gather wild onions, dig potatoes, or catch the fish—unless you want to!

INGREDIENTS

2 cups raw potatoes, cut in cubes
3 cups water
1 pound fresh or frozen fish fillets, cut in 2-inch pieces
Salt and pepper
1 tablespoon oil
½ cup onion, chopped
2 cups milk
3 tablespoons flour

Native Wisdom *Many tribes were like the Spokane people who had a Salmon Chief, in charge of fishing. He told the tribe when and where they could fish. Anyone who disobeyed him was punished. This helped control the food supply and kept people from taking all the fish.*

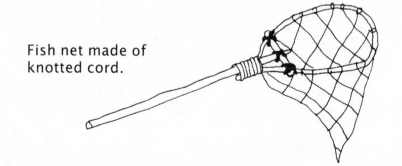

Fish net made of knotted cord.

UTENSILS

Large pot with lid
Small frying pan
Spoons

Bring the water to a low boil in the pot and cook the potatoes in it for 5 minutes. Add the fish to the potatoes and sprinkle with salt and pepper. Put the lid on the pot, turn down the heat, and simmer for 10 minutes.

Put the oil in a frying pan, add the onion, and fry it until it's golden. Add it to the soup. Mix the milk and flour together, stirring to break up any lumps, and add it to the soup. Cook and stir a few minutes until the soup thickens.

Staying Alive In the winter, rivers and streams froze and people couldn't fish. If they hadn't saved enough food to last through the winter, they made soup out of the black moss that grows on pine trees and ate the inner bark of trees to keep from starving.

Fish trap made from a basket.

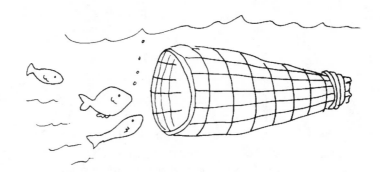

Boiled Eggs

Plains people gathered wild bird's eggs in the spring. To cook them, they dug a hole, filled it with water, and set the eggs on a rack of sticks above the water. Red-hot stones from the campfire were rolled into the water to heat it. Grass and twigs were laid over the top to hold in the heat while the eggs cooked.

You can boil eggs in a pot of water, or put them in a covered baking dish full of water and bake in a 350°F oven for 20 minutes.

> **Native Wisdom** *There was a lot of food along the Northwest Coast. People living there ate fish, clams, deer, and wild fruits and berries. Kwakiutl women knew about 150 recipes by memory.*

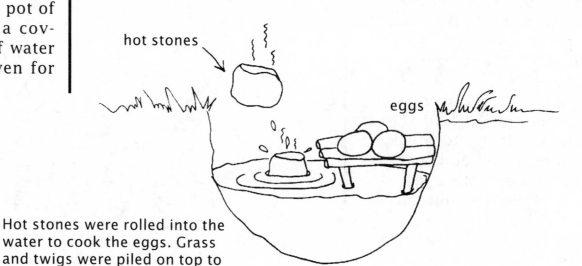

hot stones

eggs

Hot stones were rolled into the water to cook the eggs. Grass and twigs were piled on top to keep the heat in.

Popped Corn

Since most Indians ate only one or two big meals a day, they got hungry between meals. Anyone could help him- or herself to the soup or stew that was always cooking, but Indian children also ate many other snacks.

In fact, Indians created and introduced settlers to many of the snacks we eat today. Have you eaten popcorn, fruit leather, beef jerky, or roasted sunflower seeds? Those were given to us by early Indian cooks.

When Columbus came to the New World he found Indians growing more than 200 different kinds of corn. The Indians called it "maize." They ate it boiled, roasted, or ground into flour for bread. Columbus took maize seeds with him back to Europe so that people could grow it there, too.

Indians popped corn in baskets over the fire or on hot stones. You can use a popcorn popper or pop it on the stove. Put ¼ cup popcorn and 2 tablespoons oil in a large frying pan. Put on the lid and heat at medium-high heat. Ask for grown-up help when you are using hot oil. Shake the pan back and forth while it cooks to keep the kernels from sticking and burning. When the popping stops, remove the lid and put the popcorn in a large bowl.

Good Idea *Huron Indians made a snack out of maple syrup poured over popped corn—the first caramel corn!*

Roasted Pumpkin Seeds

Lay the seeds you've saved from a pumpkin on a cookie sheet to dry. When they're dry, put them in a bowl with a few tablespoons of salad oil, and mix them well so that the seeds are covered with oil. Sprinkle on some salt. Spread the seeds out on a cookie sheet and bake at 250°F until they begin to turn brown.

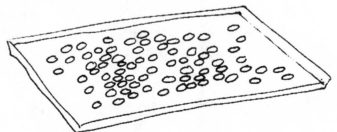

Beef Jerky

After hunters brought home deer, elk, or buffalo, the people would feast on the fresh meat. They also needed to save meat for times when hunting would be difficult, so they dried some. It was cut in long strips and hung on racks made out of poles and sticks. The meat was left in the fresh sunny air until it was dry, and then it was packed away or ground up into "pemmican." Pemmican was made from pounded jerky and mashed dried berries mixed with melted fat and formed into flat bars. It could be saved for years without spoiling. Indians brought pemmican on hunting trips for quick and easy eating.

Staying Alive *One-half pound of pemmican was enough nourishment for a person all day. This made it perfect for hunting trips and travel.*

You can make jerky at home. Use lean cuts of beef. ("Lean" means that the meat doesn't have fat on it.) Use a frozen beef round steak because it's easier to cut frozen. Ask an adult to help you cut off all the fat, and then slice it into narrow strips about ¼ inch thick and 1 inch wide. Sprinkle salt on both sides. Use a heavy needle (like a carpet needle) to string the meat on heavy thread. Space the pieces evenly so that they don't touch each other.

Use thumbtacks to hang it across a corner of a room or porch. You can hang it in a warm place, like over a fireplace, in the winter. It will take several days to dry.

You can also make beef jerky in the oven. Put a layer of meat strips in a bowl and sprinkle them with salt and "liquid smoke," which you can purchase at a grocery store or sporting goods shop. Continue layering meat, salt, and liquid smoke. Cover and put into the refrigerator overnight. Drain the strips on paper towels and pat them dry. Lay the strips on a rack in a baking pan, and bake in the oven at 250°F for about 3½ hours, until the meat is dry.

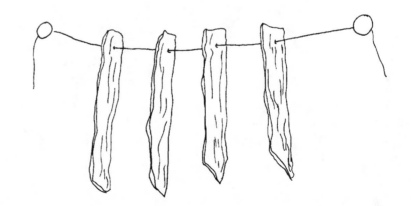

Fruit Leather

Indian people picked and ate various kinds of wild berries—strawberries, blueberries, wild grapes, cranberries, and many more. They learned what berry plants looked like, where to find them, and when to pick them every year.

Berries were carried home in baskets and eaten fresh, but they were also dried and saved for the winter.

You can make a dried fruit snack for yourself using fresh or frozen berries.

Depending on Plants
Native Americans picked 36 different wild fruits that they dried to eat in the winter.

Good Manners *If Yurok children, who lived in California, talked or ate too fast, their parents silently took away their food basket and the children had to quietly leave the house.*

INGREDIENTS

2 cups of ripe fruit
(berries, cherries, plums, apricots, peaches, apples, or a mixture of these)

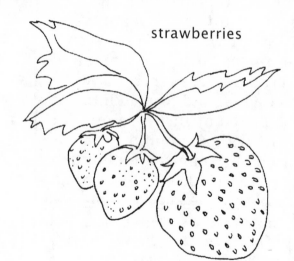

strawberries

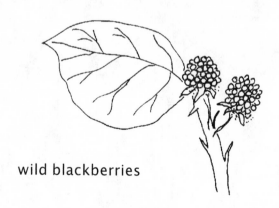

wild blackberries

UTENSILS

Table knife
Blender
Cookie sheet
Plastic wrap
Wooden spoon

Mix the fruit in a blender.

Wash the fruit and let it drain. Cut it into small chunks. Leave the peels—they are chewy and nutritious. Put the fruit in the blender and blend for 15 seconds. (Count to 15 slowly.) Pour the mixture out onto a cookie sheet lined with plastic wrap. Let it dry in a warm place for a day or so.

To eat, peel the fruit off the plastic wrap. You can roll it up in the plastic wrap and keep it in a covered container to store.

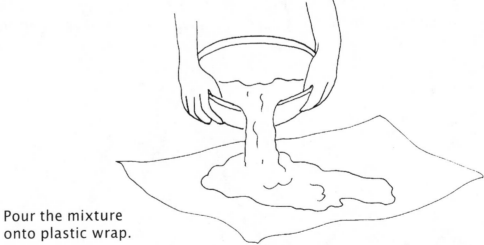

Pour the mixture
onto plastic wrap.

Raisins

Indians picked wild grapes and ate them fresh or dried them. Dried grapes were added to stews. Grape leaves were soaked in water and used to cure many illnesses, from snakebite to diarrhea. Grapevines were used to weave baskets.

You can dry grapes to make raisins.

To make your own raisins, you will need some fresh grapes. Use the seedless kind. Wash them in a basin. Lay waxed paper on cookie sheets and spread the grapes on the paper. Set them out in the sun; a table on a deck or porch works nicely. It will take several days for them to dry into raisins. You may want to turn them over a few times while they are drying.

You can make raisins faster in the oven. Heat the oven to 170°F. Lay the grapes on a cookie sheet (no waxed paper), and leave them in the oven for 24 hours (all day and all night). Then you'll have raisins!

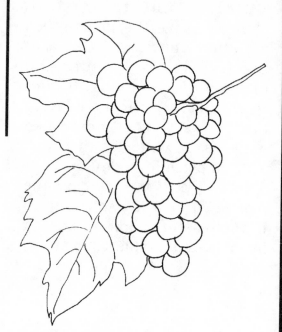

Dry in the warm sun.

Peanut Butter

Indians gathered all sorts of nuts—acorns, hickory nuts, pecans, butternuts, hazelnuts, black walnuts, and pine nuts. They also grew sunflowers for the seeds, which they roasted in baskets with hot coals.

Nuts were sometimes ground up with stones and pressed into cakes.

Peanuts were grown by Native American farmers on the Caribbean Islands when Columbus arrived. He'd never seen them before.

You can make your own peanut butter that is similar to the nutty pastes some tribes made.

Ask a grown-up to help you with the blender. Put everything in the blender. Blend with the lid on at medium speed for a few seconds. Stop and use the spoon to push the nuts back down the sides of the blender. Continue blending, stopping to stir when needed, until it is a creamy paste. Spread it on bread. Native Americans enjoyed wild honey when they could find it—add a bit of honey to your own peanut butter.

INGREDIENTS

1 cup shelled peanuts
3 tablespoons vegetable oil
½ teaspoon of salt

UTENSILS

Blender
Long-handled spoon

Depending on Plants People in California gathered and ground up acorns to make bread and mush to eat. They used a special method of soaking and rinsing the acorns to take away the bitter taste and the poisonous tannic acid.

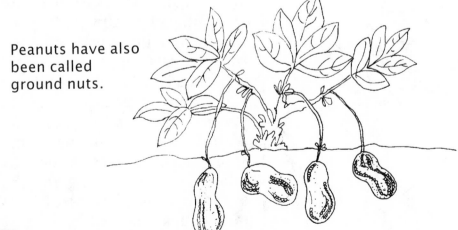

Peanuts have also been called ground nuts.

Maple Sugar Candy

Sap from maple trees dripped down sticks and into birch bark buckets.

The Chippewa people who lived near the Great Lakes made sugar and maple syrup from the sap of maple trees.

Each year, usually in March, they went to the maple camp. They walked over the snow in snowshoes and carried rolls of birch bark on their backs. They used the bark to repair the roofs of the little huts at the sugar camp. Dogs pulled sleds piled with children and belongings. They went to the same sugar camp every year and stored bark pans and wooden buckets there to use each year. A bark pan could sometimes last 10 years.

Long ago, Indians discovered that maple trees have a sweet sap that can be drained from the tree and boiled to make syrup and sugar. They used an ax to make a cut in the maple tree's bark. A short stick was pushed in the opening and the sap ran down the stick and into a bucket below.

The sap was boiled over the fire until it became thick and grainy and could be pounded into sugar.

Chippewa mothers made maple candy for their children by folding little cones of thin birch bark and filling them with sugar. They also made molded candies. First, they carved the shapes of animals, moons, and stars into wooden molds. Then, they pressed soft sugar into the molds. When the sugar hardened, they wrapped it in thin pieces of birch bark.

You can make an easy maple-tasting candy. This recipe makes about 30 candies.

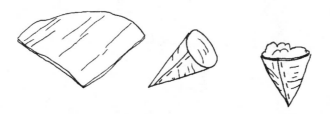

Thin pieces of birch bark were stitched into small cones that held maple sugar treats.

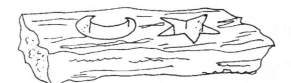

Candy molds were carved from wood.

Maple candies were molded into different shapes.

INGREDIENTS

⅓ cup margarine, softened
⅓ cup maple-flavored
pancake syrup
½ teaspoon salt
1 pound powdered sugar

UTENSILS

Large bowl
Spoon
Cookie sheet
(covered with aluminum foil
for easy cleanup)
Plastic candy molds, if you like

Put the margarine, syrup, and salt in the bowl and mix with the spoon. Mix in the sugar. When it gets difficult to stir, use your hands to knead it until it is a smooth dough. Add more sugar if the dough sticks to your hands. Roll 1-inch balls and let them harden on the cookie sheet. If you want to make molded candies, press the mixture into the plastic candy molds. Pop out the forms and let them harden on a cookie sheet. These are a fondant-type candy, which means that they won't get really hard.

You can dip the balls in melted chocolate or roll them in coconut, chopped nuts, or dry cereal, if you like.

Shape your candies by rolling
them into balls or pressing them
into plastic molds.

Good Idea *Long ago, Indian children dripped maple syrup over scoops of ice for a tasty treat—the first snow cones!*

Drinks

Thirsty children usually drank icy cold water from mountain streams or rivers. They also had special drinks now and then.

Maple syrup was mixed with water to make a punch.

Leaves were used to flavor drinks, too. The dried leaves of snowberry, wintergreen, and spruce and twigs of raspberry, and other wild plants were tied and dropped into boiling water to make tea. Flowers were dried and added to tea, too.

Wild mint leaves were gathered and used to flavor teas and punch.

You can make a punch like the Indian children enjoyed during hot summer days. Pour a glass of fruit juice and add a squirt of honey and a fresh mint leaf. Stir and enjoy!

Depending on Plants *Many times an Indian medicine man would fix a tea out of crushed mint leaves in water. Try it yourself; it's tasty!*

Staying Alive *Maple syrup was also used to sweeten medicines made from bitter plants, so the children would eat them. Just like some medicine today.*

fresh mint leaf

PASS IT ON—TELL SOMEONE

There are many ways to pass a message on to someone else. We use phones, faxes, TV, radio, newspapers, and even skywriting! Many years ago Native Americans found creative ways to communicate with others, too. We have no way to know what Indian ancestors really said to each other because they left no written records. However, we have "petroglyphs"—Indian carvings and etchings in stone.

Puzzling Petroglyphs

Petroglyphs are designs carved into stone. In the Southwest—Utah, Colorado, Arizona and New Mexico—there are many places where you can still find these designs on smooth rock. They were made over a thousand years ago by the ancestors of today's Native Americans.

The artists who made them used stones to chip away the rock, creating pictures of people, animals, the sun, the moon, stars, and other designs. Petroglyphs are certainly puzzles from the past. We don't know what the designs meant, or why they were carved.

You can make a petroglyph like the ancient people did.

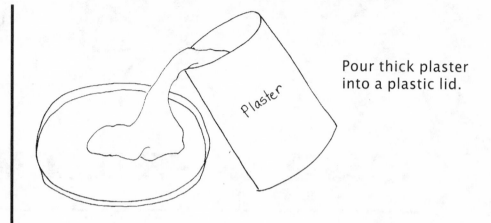

Pour thick plaster into a plastic lid.

Insert a paper clip so that you can hang it up later.

Carve a picture in the plaster.

MATERIALS

Plaster of paris
Water
Container for mixing plaster
Stick or spoon
for mixing plaster
Flat, plastic lid from coffee or
shortening can, or
aluminum foil
Paper clip (optional)
Carving tool
(pencil, old ballpoint pen,
stick, or sharp stone)
Tempera paints, watercolors,
or shoe polish
Acrylic floor wax

Mix the plaster and water following the directions on the plaster package. When it begins to thicken, pour some onto the lid until it's covered. If you are using foil, spoon or pour the plaster to make a thick plaster pancake on the foil.

If you want to hang your petroglyph on the wall, push a paper clip into the plaster before it hardens. Later you can hang it from a nail.

Let the plaster harden, and then peel away the foil or lid. Use your carving tool to scratch a picture or design in the plaster.

When it's finished, you can paint the plaster with tempera or watercolors, or rub shoe polish over it with a cloth rag. Brush on a coat of acrylic floor wax to give it a shiny finish.

Here are some designs
the ancestors made.
What do you think each
one means?
Copy them or make up
your own!

Pictographs

Put on the shirt or apron to protect your clothing. Protect your table top from paint splatters with old newspaper. This project is great for outdoors—use the ground or a picnic table.

Squirt blobs of paint onto the paper. Then, blow air through the straw to splatter the paint. Push the wet paint around on the paper by blowing air on it. *Don't suck the paint up into the straw.*

Use several different colors to see what effects you can create.

When your spatter painting is dry, use it as gift wrap or fold it to make note cards. You can also try drawing over it with ink or markers or gluing on bits of torn papers.

Blow air through a straw to move the paint on the paper.

MATERIALS

Tempera paints
Shelf paper or newsprint
Drinking straw
Old shirt or apron
Newspapers

Pictographs are paintings that were done on rocks or cave walls over a thousand years ago.

The artists used ground-up clay, sand, plant dyes mixed with blood, eggs, and tree sap.

The first artists painted with their fingers. Later, they made brushes from animal hair or plant stems. Some of them spattered paint by blowing through a hollow reed.

Try finger painting or experiment with spatter painting, following these directions.

Sign Language

The Indian peoples of North America spoke over 300 different languages. Many of the tribes traveled and traded with other tribes who didn't speak their language. How could they talk to each other? They invented a silent way of speaking with their hands.

Sign language seems to have developed on the Plains. The Kiowa, Sioux, Arapaho, Cheyenne, and Blackfoot understood and used sign talk with each other.

Using silent hand signals also came in handy when hunters tried to sneak up on a buffalo herd. They could signal each other without making a sound that might scare the animals away.

Indians used sign language to speak with traders or to make treaties between warring tribes.

Sign language is a bit different than spoken words. To ask a question, you must make the sign that means "question" first. Use the sign for "question" for the words: what, where, why, and when.

If you want to ask "What is your name?" you make the sign "question," then "you," then "called."

"How old are you?" becomes "question," "how many," "you," "winter." (Many tribes kept track of the years by counting the winters.)

"I'm going home" becomes "I," "go," "house."

> **Fast Fact** In 1885, there were more than 110,000 sign-talking Indians in the United States.
>
> **Fast Fact** Two hundred years ago, there were at least 600 tribes in North America that spoke 300 languages.

"I'm going home" is signed like this:

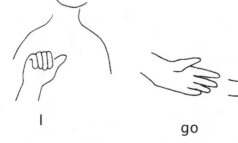

I   go   house

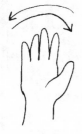

Wave your hand back and forth to make the sign for "question."

To ask "What is your name?" make signs for "question," "you," and "called."

question

you

called

To ask "How old are you?" make signs for "question," "how many," "you," and "winter."

question

how many

you

winter

Totem Poles

Totem poles still stand tall outside native homes and in special parks in the Northwest. They were a special sign that people put up outside their homes.

The only Indians to make totem poles lived in the Northwest Coast area, from southern Alaska to the Seattle, Washington, area. Because there was plenty of food along the coast, the Indians that lived there had more time to explore art than other tribes. There is a story that says that the first totem pole floated in from the sea. The totem nations were Tlinget, Haida, Kwakiutl, Nootka, Salish, Tsimsyan, and Bella Coola. Each nation was divided into tribes, then clans, and then related families. The Haidas were the first to make totem poles.

Totem poles weren't part of Indian religion but simply told the life story of their owners. A pole told the stories of a man's or family's history and special deeds, or preserved old tales that grandparents had handed down. Carvers often used animal and human figures to tell these stories.

Every man wanted his own totem pole, and the higher the pole the more important the person. Feuds often started when chiefs tried to outdo each other with taller totem poles.

To make a pole, a red cedar tree was cut down, towed to a stream, and floated to the village. Early carving tools were made of stone and bone, but later traders brought iron tools that worked better. Designs were painted with animal oils and blood, salmon eggs, charcoal, graphite, ocher, and moss. Paint brushes were made of animal fur.

Carvers tried to create beautiful and original carvings—no carver wanted to be a copycat. They were selected from the best craftsmen and they worked on the pole at a secret location. One group of carvers, the Tsimsyan, killed anyone caught spying on them. Also, one of them could be put to death if he made a serious mistake when carving! When the pole was complete, it was brought to the village and a big ceremony was held as it was put up.

Totem poles were never sold between Indians because no one had any interest in owning a pole with another family's history.

> **Fast Fact** If one chief wanted to embarrass another in order to collect an unpaid debt, he would order the other chief's figure carved upside down on a "shame" pole for everyone to see.

Make a totem pole to put on your desk or dresser.

MATERIALS

Cardboard egg carton
Tempera paint
Scissors
Glue

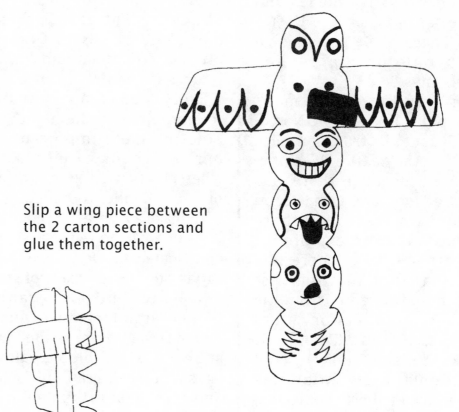

Cut the lid off the carton. Cut the egg cup section in half lengthwise and trim the rough edges away. Cut fins for salmon and wings for an eagle from the flat section of the carton.

Glue together the 2 egg cup sections, back-to-back, with the wing slipped in between. Paint different faces and symbols.

Slip a wing piece between the 2 carton sections and glue them together.

You can work with friends to create a large totem pole for your classroom or clubhouse.

Glue boxes and cans together to make a large totem pole.

MATERIALS

Several boxes and large cans
Rock or brick
Tub and tile caulk (or hot glue gun with grown-up help)
Tempera or leftover latex house paint
Brushes

 Position the larger boxes or cans at the bottom. Put a rock or brick inside the bottom one to weigh it down. Glue 1 box on top of another with the caulk. When the glue hardens, paint the boxes to create whales, beavers, bears, or whatever you choose.

Fast Fact *The common symbols on totem poles are the bird, snake, halibut, frog, beaver, bear, killer whale, seal, and thunderbird.*

Sandpainting

Navajo sandpainters of the Southwest painted special paintings on the ground with colored sands. These paintings were used for curing sickness or praying. They were not done for enjoyment, but as a religious ceremony.

Sand, flower pollen, and charcoal were trickled onto smooth sand. The design might ask a cure for a sick child, who would sit on the sandpainting during the curing ceremony.

At sunset, the sandpainting was scattered so that evil spirits would not come.

This is a fun project! You can make several quick and easy sandpaintings to hang on your wall.

Make your colored "sand" by putting 2 tablespoons of cornmeal in a cup, squirting food coloring on it, and mixing it up. Add more drops of coloring if you want it darker. Make several different colors to use.

Squirt the glue onto the paper in any design you like. Sprinkle the colored cornmeal onto the wet glue. Shake the excess cornmeal back into the jar so that you can use it again.

Squirt on more glue and sprinkle a different color of cornmeal. Shake off all the loose cornmeal and let your painting dry.

MATERIALS

Cornmeal
Construction paper, black or another dark color,
6 by 6 inches
Food coloring
Small jars or cups
White glue

Squirt glue in a design on the paper. Sprinkle the cornmeal onto the glue. Shake off the excess meal and let dry.

Mix the cornmeal and food coloring.

Winter Count

Dakota and Kiowa people of the Plains kept track of their history with a calendar they drew on deer, antelope, or buffalo hides. They wrote with charcoal, plant dyes, or paints made from crushed clay and animal fat.

They drew pictures to remind them of battles, hunts, hungry winters, births, deaths, and other special things that happened.

Native Americans counted their ages by how many winters they had seen. The Dakota drew a picture for each year's winter so that they could count years as they passed.

Sometimes an artist would record a special hunt or battle on a hide. It was rolled up, saved, and passed on to grandchildren so that they could learn about the event.

You can make one on a large paper, drawing symbols with markers or paints. Draw pictures to record all the things that have happened since you were born. How many winter symbols will you need to draw?

grass

deer

turtle

day

Can you match these up?

MATERIALS

Old bed sheet or
large brown paper bag
Raw potatoes, sponges,
or pink erasers
Tempera paints
Fine-point markers

Cut the sheet or bag into an animal hide shape. Cut the potatoes, sponges, and erasers into shapes of buffalo, elk, or horses. Use the tempera paint to stamp them on the "hide." Draw the hunters or warriors.

> **Native Wisdom** *Chippewa people kept records on sheets of birch bark that were taken out and read every 15 years. If a piece started to wear out it was recopied onto fresh bark. The stories on the bark told how to worship and what sort of life one should live.*

Here are some symbols the Sioux used.
Go ahead and make up some for your own story!

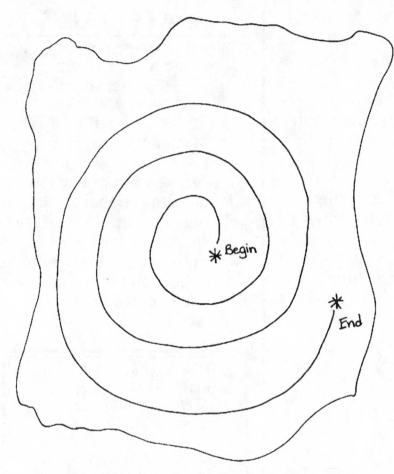

* Begin

* End

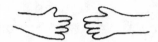

A handshake told of a
peace between the tribes.

A horse told of successful
pony raids.

Arrows hitting a tepee told
of attacks by other tribes.

The Dakota Sioux winter counts began in the center
and the pictures were drawn in an spiral. The painted
pictures on the buffalo hide became a calendar, history, and work of art. Some winter counts were written over a period of 70 years. People would pass them
on to their children and grandchildren so that they
could add to the story.

Smoke Signals

What did smoke signals mean?

1 puff meant "attention."

2 puffs meant "everything's OK."

3 puffs meant "Danger!" or "Help!"

Long before telephones, Indians had thought of a way to signal each other across miles of plains and prairie. They used the smoke from a fire to send messages across the land.

The proper fire was important. They built a small fire, and then piled on damp grass. This created a lot of smoke. Two people would stretch a blanket or animal hide over the fire and lift it up to send a cloud of smoke up into the air.

The Apaches would build several fires at once for sending alarm or danger signals.

Practice sending signals to a friend with flashlights in the dark. The signal of 3 flashes usually means help. Make up some signals in a secret code for you and a friend to use.

Story Stick

Some people, like the Pima of Arizona, kept records of things that had happened in their lives on story sticks. These were smooth, flat sticks with pictures drawn or burned onto them. They were decorated with paint and wrapped with sinew and feathers.

Make one for yourself.

> **Native Wisdom** *Everyone in the Iroquois group of tribes could vote, even the children. If they were too young to vote, their mothers did it for them. The Pacific Northwest tribes also allowed children to discuss issues in tribal meetings.*

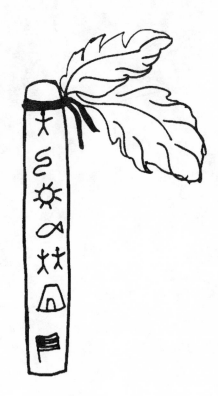

MATERIALS

Tongue depressor
Fine-point permanent markers
Yarn scraps
2 or 3 feathers
(real or cut from paper or felt)

You will need 1 tongue depressor for each story.

Plan your story first, sketching it on scrap paper.

Draw the first part of your story at the top of the stick. Continue making drawings down the stick, showing each thing that happened next.

When you are finished, wrap a piece of yarn around 1 end and knot it tightly. Tie a feather or 2 onto the ends of the yarn.

Owner Sticks

MATERIALS

2½-inch sticks or dowels, one
1 foot long and one 2 feet long
Heavy twine
Feathers
(real or cut from paper)
Felt or fake fur strips
Yarn scraps
Pocket knife
(with grown-up help)
Black plastic tape (optional)
Glue

Good Manners *If a person made a mistake, a gentle joke was made to point it out to them, instead of a reprimand.*

 Have an adult help carve away a bit of the longer stick where it meets the shorter one to form a cross. This will help the sticks lie flat.

Wrap the twine around the 2 sticks to hold them together and knot it securely.

Decorate your stick with markers or paint. You can wind black plastic tape around the dowel in a spiral.

People in many tribes made owner sticks to show that something belonged to them. When they stuck the stick in the ground next to a pile of firewood they had gathered or a freshly killed deer, it showed anyone passing by that it belonged to someone.

Each person or family created a special design and decorated their stick so that it was different from anyone else's. They made several sticks so they always had extras to mark things with.

Make your own owner stick to prop against the wall of your room, to save yourself a spot at a picnic, or to lay across your favorite chair when you leave it to get a snack.

Tie on pieces of fabric and yarn tassels.
Decorate with colored tape or brightly colored paint.

Make yarn tassels: Wrap yarn around cardboard. Tie one end securely. Cut the other ends.

Birch Bark Transparencies

MATERIALS

Typing, copier, or recycled paper
Construction paper
Hole punch

Fold the paper into squares, rectangles, or triangles. Punch holes in any design you choose. Unfold to see what it looks like.

Practice with several different designs. When you find some you like, glue them to large pieces of colored construction paper. You can fold them to make greeting cards or use them as placemats.

Native Wisdom *The moons (or months) had names.*
January = Snow Moon
February = Hunger Moon
March = Crow Moon
April = Grass Moon
May = Planting Moon
June = Rose Moon
July = Heat Moon
August = Thunder Moon
September = Hunting Moon
October = Falling Leaf Moon
November = Beaver Moon
December = Long Night Moon
Why do you think each month was called as it was?

Chippewa girls found an unusual way to create artwork from thin pieces of birch bark.

They folded the bark several times, and then used their teeth to punch holes in it.

When they unfolded the bark, a pretty or interesting pattern of holes appeared.

They especially enjoyed making these during the long winter nights when they would hold the punched bark up by the fire and see the light flicker through the holes in the pattern.

They tried to make each bark design different, never copying another.

Indians made designs on birch bark with their teeth. Can you make the same designs from paper with a hole punch? Make up some new designs of your own!

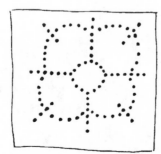
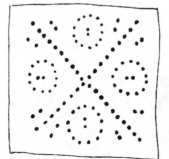
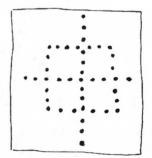

Talking Feather

Some tribes used a "talking feather" during storytelling or discussions. A decorated feather was passed around the circle, and whoever held it was the only one allowed to speak. This prevented interruptions and gave people as much time as they needed to say what was on their mind.

Make your own talking feather to use for family meetings or in your club or classroom.

> **Native Wisdom** *Native American people believe strongly in giving people the chance to make up their own minds or express themselves without being told what to do.*

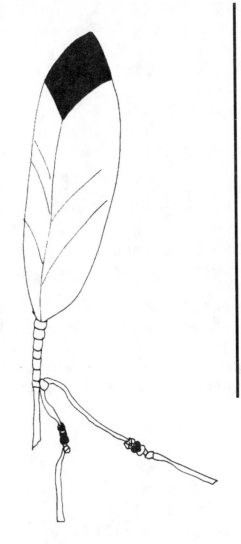

MATERIALS

1 large turkey feather
(buy at a craft supply store if you can't find one)
Beads
Thin piece of leather bootlace or ¼-inch ribbon
Glue

Wrap the feather with the lacing or ribbon. Glue the ends in place to hold it. Tie on another piece of ribbon. String beads on the ends of the ribbon and knot the ends so that they don't fall off.

You can decorate your feather any way you choose, even coloring it with marking pens if you like.

Storytelling

Telling stories was popular with all Native American tribes. A favorite storyteller or the chief often would tell stories about the tribe's past or explain religious beliefs. Adults and children enjoyed listening to stories, just as we do now. They told stories for entertainment during long winters and to pass on the beliefs and values of the people. Children were taught many stories, and they kept them in their memory to share with their own children.

Stories from Europe that we call fairy tales begin with "once upon a time." Indian myths often begin with "before the people came."

Storytelling was a special activity, and it had different rules for each tribe. The White Mountain Apaches told stories only between dusk and dawn and when it was cold.

Indians liked to use stories to teach lessons about how to act and live with others. They also used stories in healing ceremonies.

You can enjoy storytelling, too. Make up a story with a friend by taking turns telling parts of the story. You can also tell a story and then try to remember the same exact story and tell it again the next night. Get your parents to tell stories about when they were children or about you when you were much younger.

> ***Native Wisdom*** *A television is only entertainment—a story is much more.*
>
> ***Fast Fact*** *Indian storytelling wasn't just for children. Some stories were so important they could only be told by certain people at certain times.*

Storytelling Bag

Iroquois storytellers used a special bag full of props. They would take out a toy or doll and hold it up as they began their story. Make one yourself. Decorate a paper lunch bag with crayons or markers. Look for interesting things you can make up stories about and put them in the bag. Use stones, feathers, fossils, or small toys. Practice stories to go with each item.

Storytellers would keep the audience interested by saying "Ho?" and the audience would answer "Hey!" Try it while you tell your tales.

Iroquois storytellers were given a gift when they were finished telling a story. The storyteller would spend the night with the family, and then travel on to the next house in the morning.

Decorate a storytelling bag to hold the items you will use when telling stories.

Cherokee Alphabet

Sikwayi (also called Sequoyah or Sequoia) was the son of a British trader and a Cherokee woman. He felt that if the Cherokee people had more knowledge they would be able to remain independent. In 1821, when settlers were taking over the West and crowding Indians off of their land, he made up an alphabet with 86 symbols—one for each sound in the Cherokee language. The Cherokee people learned it quickly, even though they didn't have schools. People could learn the alphabet in one day and could read a book written in it in less than a week. They began publishing books and newspapers in their own language. Some Cherokee people today still learn this language.

The giant redwood tree in California was named after Sequoia to honor the Cherokee teacher.

Cherokee Alphabet.

D a		R e	T i	ꭰ o	O u	i v	
S ga	Ꭳ ka	Ᏺ ge	Ᏹ gi	A go	J gu	E gv	
Ꮤ ha		Ꭾ he	Ꭿ hi	F ho	Ꮁ hu	Ꭹ hv	
W la		Ꮈ le	Ꭴ me	G lo	M lu	Ꮜ lv	
Ꮉ ma		Ꮃ me	Λ ne	ꭵ mo	Ᏽ mu	O nv	
Θ na	Ꮏ hna	Ꮐ nah	Ꮃ que	Z no	Ꮒ nu	Ꮕ quv	
Ꭲ qua		ꭴ que	ꭷ qui	Ꮩ quo	Ꮔ quu	R sv	
Ꮓ sa	Ꮝ s	4 se	Ꮖ si	Ꮈ so	Ꮪ su	Ꮫ dv	
Ꮣ da	W ta	Ꮥ de Ꮦ te	Ꭵ di Ꮧ ti	V do	S du	P tlv	
Ꮪ dla	L tla	L tle	C tli	Ꮱ tlo	Ꮲ tlu	C tsv	
Ꮳ tsa		Ꮴ tse	Ꮵ tsi	K tso	J tsu	6 wv	
Ꮤ wa		Ꮾ we	Ꮎ wi	Ꮼ wo	Ꮻ wu	B yv	
Ꮿ ya		β ye	ꮿ yi	Ꮀ yo	Ꮐ yu		

GV   thank you

ii   yes

ꓕꟼ   one

Wꟼ   two

KT   three

Navajo Code Talkers

Navajo "code talkers" in World War II sent messages the Japanese couldn't figure out. More than 330 Navajos were carefully trained in sending coded messages that explained where troops were located and called for help during battles.

These soldiers were good in both English and Navajo languages. Letters of the alphabet were given new names and then were changed to Navajo words. The code talkers could speak in this code over radio or telephone, and no one could understand what they were saying.

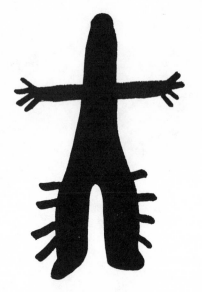

INDIAN CHILDHOOD

What was it like then? What is it like now? In some ways life was very different for Indian children long ago. They had to find food and things to make clothes from. They had to make everything they owned, or make things to trade for what they couldn't make.

They didn't go to school; instead, they learned everything they needed to know by working alongside grown-ups.

Some tribes traveled and they saw a lot of country. Other people lived in the same village their whole lives and never saw a different place.

Children had to walk everywhere they went. There were no horses until the Spaniards brought them on ships to Mexico, and it took many years for runaway horses to become the large herds the tribes needed. Many tribes never did have horses.

Indian babies were carried in cradleboards. They were strapped to the boards so they could be taken everywhere their mother went. They could be hung on their mother's back or from a saddle or tree branch. The baby could look at tiny toys or clay animals hung on a string from the hoop over her or his head. These charms served as spirit protectors that made the baby safe and strong.

Babies didn't wear diapers. Instead, soft dry moss and fluff from cattails was wrapped around them in the cradleboard. It was changed whenever it got dirty.

Children were kept very clean. The Gros Ventre children of Montana were awakened before dawn, summer and winter, and bathed. Tlingit children of the Northwest Coast bathed at dawn every day in cold water. Children who lived in the dry deserts of the Southwest had no water to spare for baths, so they were rubbed clean with sand each day. Most children living in warm areas didn't wear clothing until they were five or six years old; then they wore clothing styles just like their parents.

Children younger than five or six years stayed with the women all day, helping to gather wild foods, firewood, water, and delivering messages. They played with small tools, dolls, and canoes that grown-ups made for them. Wolves and coyotes were often tamed as pets for the children.

Children between six and 11 years old divided into boy and girl groups for play and work.

Jicarilla Apache girls learned to gather food, grind corn, and ride and care for horses. Salish girls built playhouses and little salmon traps in the streams. They learned craft skills from older women. A girl's first bags and baskets were proudly hung on trees along the village trails so everyone could view them. Girls also learned how to skin and cure animal hides, furnish the house, and make clothing, pots, and baskets for their family. A Salish girl's first roots and fruits were celebrated with a family ceremony. The foods were served by the girl to her relatives.

Girls also learned to do well in sports because it made them strong and fast. They had swimming races and foot races, rode horseback, and played ball games. Chippewa girls learned to net fish and trap small animals with their fathers.

Boys in every tribe needed to learn to fish and hunt. They never did "women's work." They made and played with small spears, sling shots, bows and arrows, and blow guns. They made and learned to walk in snowshoes and practiced riding horses.

To make them stronger, boys were often given ice cold baths and required to endure harsh conditions.

They practiced their hunting skills, bringing home meat for their family and the village as often as they could. Boys enjoyed many sports, and games that made them strong and fast for hunting.

Children were treated with love by everyone in the tribe. They were never spanked or hit. Indian grown-ups believed that if a child was hit, his or her spirit might be broken. Naughty children might have to miss a meal for punishment. In some tribes, parents made up stories about an old witch that would punish bad children in order to scare the children if they didn't behave.

Children of long ago worked hard and grew up fast. Boys and girls were ready to be married by the time they were 15 years old. Most marriages were arranged by their families or by the tribe.

Life is different today. Native American children's lives are very much like other children's. They go to school and movies, and play sports. Some live in the country on reservations, which are large areas of land owned by the tribe. Others live in cities or small towns. Their homes, food, and clothing are like their neighbors'.

While Native American people don't want to live in the past, they are very proud of their history and try to preserve their religions and customs. They enjoy teaching them to their children so that the culture won't be forgotten.

Many Indian children today speak their tribal language and English, too. They play video games, and they also know the old dances. They eat ice cream and fry bread. They ride bikes more often than horses. They are learning old ways and new ways as they grow up.

It can be wonderful and very useful to know both old ways and new ways. This book can help you enjoy the old ways, even as you explore them in all kinds of new ways, often by combining traditional methods and designs with some of today's materials and tools.

If you have already done the projects in this book, why not go back and do them again in different ways? Each time you pick up this book and make something, such as a clay pot or a musical instrument, and every time you use the pot or play the instrument, you can learn a little more about traditional North American Indian life. Have fun!

Bibliography

Billard, Jules B., ed. *The World of the American Indian.* Washington, D.C.: National Geographic Society, 1979.

Branson, Oscar T. *Fetishes and Carvings of the Southwest.* Tucson, Ariz.: Treasure Chest Publications, 1976.

Caduto, Michael, and Joseph Bruchac. *Keepers of the Earth.* Golden, Colo.: Fulcrum Publishing, 1988.

Catlin, George. *Letters and Notes on the Manners, Customs, and Conditions of North American Indians.* New York: Dover Publications, Inc., 1973. Reprint of original published in 1844.

Culin, Stewart. *Games of the North American Indians.* New York: Dover Publications, Inc., 1975.

Densmore, Frances. *How Indians Use Wild Plants for Food, Medicine and Crafts.* New York: Dover Publications, Inc., 1974.

Erdoes, Richard, and Alfonso Ortiz. *American Indian Myths and Legends.* New York: Pantheon, 1984.

Goodchild, Peter. *Survival Skills of the North American Indians.* Chicago: Chicago Review Press, 1984.

Holder, Glenn. *Talking Totem Poles.* New York: Dodd, Mead & Company, 1973.

Hunt, W. Ben. *The Complete How-to Book of Indiancraft.* New York: Macmillan Publishers, 1973.

Isaac, Barbara, ed. *Hall of the North American Indian.* Cambridge, Mass.: Peabody Museum, Harvard University Press, 1990.

Johnson, Judi. *Native American Dolls and Cradleboards, Handbook of Collections, No. 4.* Springfield, Ill.: Illinois State Museum, 1983.

Liptak, Karen. *North American Indian Sign Language.* New York: Franklin Watts Publishing, 1990.

Niethammer, Carolyn. *American Indian Food and Lore.* New York: Macmillan Publishing, 1974.

Niethammer, Carolyn. *Daughters of the Earth.* New York: Macmillan Publishing, 1977.

Palmer, Rose. *The North American Indians.* New York: Smithsonian Series Publishers, 1929, 1944.

Peltier, Jerome. *Manners and Customs of the Coeur d'Alene Indians.* Spokane, Wash.: Peltier Publications, 1975.

Salomon, Julian Harris. *The Book of Indian Crafts and Indian Lore.* New York: Harper & Row, 1928.

Stewart, Hilary. *Looking at Indian Art of the Northwest Coast.* Seattle, Wash.: University of Washington Press, 1979.

Tannahill, Reay. *Food in History.* New York: Crown Publishing, 1988.

Tomkins, William. *Indian Sign Language.* New York: Dover Publications, Inc., 1969.

Viola, Herman, and Carolyn Margolis, eds. *Seeds of Change.* Washington, D.C.: Smithsonian Institution Press, 1991.

Warner, John Anson. *Life and Art of the North American Indian.* Secaucus, N.J.: Chartwell Books, Inc., 1990.

White, Jon Manchip. *Everyday Life of the North American Indians.* New York: Dorset Press, 1979.

Whiteford, Andrew Hunter. *North American Indian Arts.* New York: Golden Press, 1990.

Williamson, Darcy, and Lisa Railsback. *Cooking With Spirit.* Bend, Ore.: Maverick Publications, 1988.

Wolfson, Evelyn. *American Indian Utensils.* New York: David McKay Company, Inc., 1979.

Wolfson, Evelyn. *Growing Up Indian.* New York: Walker & Company, 1986.